AMERICA'S FIRST BLACK POET:
JUPITER HAMMON OF LONG ISLAND

JUPITER HAMMON
FIRST PUBLISHED AFRICAN AMERICAN
POET (BORN 1711) LIVED HERE FROM
1799 UNTIL HIS DEATH IN c1806.
FIRST HOME PURCHASED BY AN AFRICAN
AMERICAN IN THE TOWN OF HUNTINGTON.
ERECTED 2016

Jupiter Hammon's Post Slave Home,
73 West Shore Road, Huntington, NY.
Photo of Historic Road Sign. Photos by
Suzanne Skidmore

AMERICA'S FIRST BLACK POET: JUPITER HAMMON OF LONG ISLAND

Edited with an Introduction by
STANLEY AUSTIN RANSOM JR.

Celebrate Black Poetry Day on October 17th

outskirts
press
2020

Outskirts Press, Inc.
http://www.outskirtspress.com

ISBN: 978-1-9772-2039-4

Library of Congress Control Number: 2020903957

Cover Design by Edith DeLaney

Outskirts Press and the "OP" logo are trademarks belonging to Outskirts Press, Inc.

PRINTED IN THE UNITED STATES OF AMERICA

Dedicated to my wife, Christina Roxane Ransom,
And to
Sarah Ransom Canino, Stanley Austin Ransom III,
Rebecca Phelps Ransom,
Shani Darden Ferrari, and their families,

And dedicated also to
Jupiter Hammon and Phillis Wheatley,
First Black American Poets
to publish their own verses

TABLE OF CONTENTS

PREFACE

WHILE THIS BOOK tells of Jupiter Hammon, the seventeenth century Long Island slave-poet, it has a further purpose, that of acting as a beacon for Black poets writing now and in the future. This beacon includes the mission of Black Poetry Day, celebrated nationally on Jupiter's birthday of October 17th, which is "to recognize the contributions Black poets have made and are making to American life and culture, and to honor Jupiter Hammon, first Black in America to publish his own verse." Black poets are encouraged to follow their dreams and express their feelings, as Jupiter did. The public is encouraged to celebrate Black Poetry Day by promoting the public readings of Black poets and by acknowledging the value of the words and works of Black poets.

Jupiter Hammon of Long Island was a literate educated Black poet at a time in the 18th century when this was a rarity. His parents were Obium and Rose, slaves of English merchant Henry Lloyd, owner of the Manor of Queen's Village on Lloyd Neck, Long Island, who brought them from Shelter Island, NY, a 3000 acre provisioning farm located between the eastern forks of Long Island. Tamero and Ibo, parents of Obium, worked at Shelter Island and were lucky to have been transported from the Caribbean island of Barbados, where 50,000 slaves worked unceasingly night and day to grow, harvest, and press sugar cane under frightful conditions. The exploding sugar cane business required that slaves be worked hard until they died, so that citizens in New England, Great Britain and Europe could enjoy the sweet product. No land was given over to producing food to feed the slaves and their owners, who set up provisioning locations elsewhere to provide food for all the island. The Henry Lloyd family were partners in the sugar trade in Barbados, but they gradually became more involved in doing business in New England and Europe and trading goods outside their Manor location.

Obium and Rose came to Queen's Village and were married in 1710. Jupiter Hammon was born on October 17, 1711 and his brother, Obediah, who took the last name of Hammond, was born in 1715. Jupiter was educated at Queen's Village and became the first Black in America to publish his own verse, detailed later.

The audience for this book about Jupiter Hammon are all who welcome new information about creative writers of the past, especially Black poets seeking examples from history. Black students will be interested in this first black poet to publish his own verse. Long Island residents have already adopted Jupiter Hammon as their own and are proud of his life and notable accomplishments which they can now read about fully. Others may like to read about a person who rose above his station in life to be honored in the United States and throughout the world.

Black Poetry Day, October 17th, is now a leading day of celebration for Black poets through the nation. It was started on October 17, 1970, and May, 1970 was the date of the publication of my first book on Jupiter Hammon, entitled, "America's First Negro Poet; The Complete Works of Jupiter Hammon of Long Island," the term "Negro" being the accepted term at the time.

This book includes all the known works of Jupiter Hammon, including the newly found "A Poem on Sickness, Death, and Funeral," 1770, and also the new "Essay on Slavery, with Justification to Divine Providence," 1786. New information about Jupiter's life, family, travels, manumission, move to Huntington Village and last years of the poet are also included for the first time.

Curiously, no personal accounts of Jupiter Hammon have been found. No records of his death in 1805 or burial, no diary or newspaper stories of the times about him, no accounts of persons who were at his lectures or preachings, or who had met him personally have been uncovered. He never married or had children. A collection of his writings was presented to the Anglican Church in Stamford, Connecticut in 1795 by Henry Lloyd, but they turned up "missing" in 1881. Are they waiting to be found? Descendants of his brother, Obediah Hammond, have been found in Huntington, Long Island, but family papers have been burned up in house fires, and no records have been found.

Many groups will find helpful information included on celebrating Black Poetry Day, now a "National Day of Observance." Here is the place to start with recognizing the contribution that Black poets have made to American life and culture.

Suggestions of the Celebration include appearances by local or national Black poets reading their works and discussion of their thoughts with support by local and state Arts Councils. Arts posters may be used to highlight the work of local or national Black poets as part of the Black Poetry Day celebrations.

For local programs there are two new musical compositions which may be used in conjunction with the poems. First is "Jupiter Hammon's Jig," an instrumental tune to command attention, with an example on YouTube. Second is a four part harmony piece, "Address to Miss Phillis Wheatley," with music composed by Canadian musician Shirley Baird, suitable for choral groups and especially Gospel Choirs. Choirs are free to use the music without charge and to use a suggested seven stanza verse or the use the complete twenty-one verses, both by Jupiter Hammon.

Plans are being made to promote the official observance of Black Poetry Day in each state, as has been done in 1985 by the State of Oregon, and in U.S. military stations abroad, which were anxious to provide our troops with positive programs in diversity.

This book is planned to bring new information about Jupiter Hammon to the world and to change popular misconceptions about Jupiter's views on slavery. Not only was he against slavery, he pointed out how whites fought for their liberty in the Revolutionary War, but forgot to include slaves who also wanted their freedom. Some writers, as will be noted, pointed out ways in which Hammon, using a veil of religious argument, actually included messages of resistance and subversity to "the brethren," his fellow slaves. Other writers have found and explained hidden messages in his poetry and prose that tell his real feelings.

Here also is an account of the background and times of the Sylvester Family, early merchants preparing the way for the Lloyd Family and other partners who created the sugar trade. The Sylvester Family came from England to Holland to connect to the huge sugar plantation at Barbados Island staffed by thousands of slaves. The need for provisioning and supplies required the purchase of Shelter Island, NY, worked by slaves who included Jupiter's forebears.

The Lloyd Family took great interest in Jupiter, to the exclusion of other slaves, who were rented out to local farmers. Jupiter was schooled with the Lloyd children, who called him "brother Jupiter." Nehemiah Bull, the teacher, was Harvard College educated and later became a minister. After Jupiter learned to read, he was voracious in his desire to read books on religious subjects, many available in Henry Lloyd's large library. His schooling would have allowed him to do certain duties on the estate, such as acting as a butler and taking care of the house for the Lloyds. The Lloyd family, as noted in the two volume "Papers of the Lloyd Family," 1927, edited by Dorothy C. Barck, took care of their own business, kept their own records and discussed with one another certain decisions relating to their business. Jupiter was not involved in any of these decisions, and was not a party to any business transactions. Occasionally he was sent on errands to collect a bill owed to the Lloyds or other simple tasks.

Jupiter was given one important job, that of caring for one of four fruit orchards, and one especially called "Jupiter's Orchard" in the letters and discussions of the Lloyd Family members. Purchases of apple, pear and other fruit trees from the famous Prince Nursery in Flatbush, New York, were discussed by members of the family from time to time, but there was no evidence that Jupiter was included in these discussions. The Lloyds discussed and practiced advanced methods of horticulture and farming, and the orchards and plantings flourished. They were a merchant and business family, and they spent much time discussing, corresponding and planning so that these activities would flourish and grow. They were especially proud of their extensive woodlands, full of large trees, and a particular large and old tree still visited by tourists today.

The first Mrs. Henry Lloyd died in 1749. While Jupiter was growing up and attending school, his activities and education was monitored by the second Mrs. Mary Pemberton Lloyd, a widow whom Henry Lloyd married in 1729 and who took an interest in Jupiter. She was a very religious person and wrote extensively of her religious feelings. She would have encouraged the teenage Jupiter to study the divine writers in the Lloyd library. After her death, her son published in 1750 a collection of her extensive writings on religion entitled "Meditations on Divine Things."

Many persons helped with the information within. Many were friends or acquaintances from my work as Director of the Huntington Public Library. I appreciated all the information I received from the many persons I have listed in the Acknowledgement section. Lastly, we can keep Jupiter's memory and poetry alive by celebrating Black Poetry Day on or near his birthday, October 17th, and remembering its mission:

"To recognize the contributions Black poets have made and are making to American life and culture, and to honor Jupiter Hammon, first Black in America to publish his own verse."

Stanley A. Ransom, Jr.

Henry Lloyd I. Portrait by John Ware after John Wollaston: courtesy of
Mrs. Orme Wilson and the Frick Art Reference Library

ACKNOWLEDGMENTS

Christina Ransom, my wife, for her suggestions and encouragement.

Jennifer Rush, author representative, Outskirts Press, for her important publication help

Teresa Schwind, Assistant Director, Huntington Public Library, Huntington, NY, for research and information and photos.

Suzanne Skidmore, Huntington, NY, for research, much information and photos.

Dr. Alexis Levitin, Distinguished Professor, English Department, PSUC, for Forward and Black Poetry Day Committee.

Dr. Tracie Church Guzzio, Honors Department, Professor, English Department, PSUC, Black Poetry Day Committee.

Shirley Baird, Educator and musician, from Kingston, Ontario, for arranging my music for "Jupiter Hammon's Jig" and "Address to Miss Phillis Wheatley" for Gospel Choir.

Robert C. Hughes, Huntington Town Historian, for information on Jupiter's later home.

Mary Johnson Bowler, Huntington, NY, a descendent of the Hammon Family.

Charla E. Bolton, AICP, NY African American Historic Designation Council, Huntington, NY, co-author of the "Migration of Jupiter Hammon and His Family" article.

The late Reginald H. Metcalf Jr., NY African American Historic Designation Council, co-author of the "Migration of Jupiter Hammon and His Family" article.

Karen Hurd Martin, for information from the Huntington Historical Society.

Dr. Susan Gibbons, Director, Sterling Memorial Library, Yale University.

Stephen Ross, Yale Library, New Haven, CT, for copies of Hammon's poem.

Jessica Becker, Public Services, Manuscripts and Archives Yale University Library.

Shaun O'Connell and Donna Wright, Studley Printing, Plattsburgh, NY. for book jacket.

Jason Crowley, Preservation Director, SPLIA (Society for the Preservation of Long Island. Antiquities), now "Preservation Long Island."

Mary Hopkins, CEF Library System staff, who created materials for Black Poetry Day

Anne Hansen, Plattsburgh State Foundation, for her support of Black Poetry Day

Sandy Branciforte, Executive Secretary, Preservation Long Island.

Jenna Wallace Coplin, PhD. CUNY, Archeologist.

Bernard J. Reverdin, Chair, Archival Committee, Old First Presbyterian Church, Huntington, NY for his information.

Dr. Tom Zoubek, Executive Director, Stamford, CT Historical Society.

Polly Vanderwaart, Parish Historian, St. John's Episcopal Church, Stamford, CT.

McCown, Julie, Texas University at Arlington, TX, for her discovery of a new Hammon poem, "Essay on Slavery".

Harriet Gerard Clark, Executive Director, Raynham Hall Museum, Oyster Bay, NY

Claire Bellerjeau, Historian, Raynham Hall Museum, for her discovery of a new Hammon poem, "Sickness, Death, Funeral".

Joanna Aiton Kerr, Manager, Services and Private Records, Provincial Archives of New Brunswick, ca.

Reverend Dr. James R. Wheeler, Rector, St. John's Episcopal Church, Stamford, CT.

Kellie Blue-McQuade, Executive Director, Carlton County Historical Society, Woodstock, New Brunswick, ca.

Lauren Brancat, Curator, Preservation Long Island.

Sarah Krautz, Preservation Director, Preservation, Long Island.

I am indebted to the above for all their information, research and services. Thank you!

Stan Ransom

FOREWORD: DR. ALEXIS LEVITIN, PLATTSBURGH STATE UNIVERSITY

JUPITER HAMMON WAS clearly a man touched by poetry. That he was able to write poems and to publish them in an era in which he was officially a slave, another man's possession, attests to his strength of character and to the strength of the Muse herself. It is a good thing to celebrate Oct. 17th, the date of Jupiter Hammons birth, and to consider this a defining date in American History. For it helps us remark upon the basic dignity of humankind, that can rise above injustice and declare its fundamental worth.

I met Stanley Ransom shortly after arriving in Plattsburgh in 1982. By 1984, we had joined forces to initiate a Black Poetry Day Celebration at SUNY-Plattsburgh, where I was a member of the English Department. Stanley had overseen and attended the first proclamation of Black Poetry Day in 1970, in Huntington, Long Island, where he was director of the Huntington Public Library. And on Oct. 17, 1971, the well-known poet June Jordan, who lived on Long Island, joined local officials in Huntington as their first guest poet and celebrant of Black Poetry Day.

In 1984, we launched our local Black Poetry Day celebration,

again with the participation of June Jordan. We have continued to ob-
serve this event here on the SUNY-Plattsburgh campus on or around
Oct. 17th every year since then. We have had the good fortune to be
joined in our celebration by truly major figures of American poetry.
In 1985, the legendary elder of Black Poetry, Gwendolyn Brooks,
travelled all the way from Chicago by train to join us for this com-
memoration. In 1988, Amiri Baraka was our guest, accompanied by
two jazz musicians. In 1991 Lucille Clifton was our celebrant. And
the following year, only six days after winning the Nobel Prize for
Literature, Derek Walcott, honoring an agreement made half a year
earlier, came to our campus and read to a crowd of over six hundred.

Perhaps the greatest shadow that lies over our nation's history
springs from its acceptance of institutionalized slavery and the shame-
ful manifestations of racism that have persisted to this day. Surely
Black Poetry Day is a fine opportunity for us to join together to honor
one of the oldest human arts and to honor the human spirit of a peo-
ple long denied the full-range of their capacities and aspirations. It is
a day for us to celebrate our shared humanity.

Dr. Alexis Levitin, Distinguished Professor,
English Department, Plattsburgh State University
Plattsburgh, NY May 6, 2018

CHAPTER 1

INTRODUCTION

Stanley Austin Ransom Jr.

AFTER FIRST MOVING to Huntington, Long Island, in 1956, as Assistant Director and later Director of the Huntington Public Library, I became aware of a slave-poet who had lived in the 1700's about five miles north of Huntington on a peninsula of land called "Lloyd Neck." From 1965 to 1970 I researched all I could find about this early Black poet and uncovered many poems, several in nearby Long Island libraries. I published my findings in May, 1970 as "America's First Negro Poet; The Complete Works of Jupiter Hammon of Long Island," by Kennikat Press of Port Washington, NY, now no longer in existance.

The first edition of "America's First Negro Poet: The complete Works of Jupiter Hammon of Long Island" has been out of print, and the second edition, issued in 1983, is an Empire State Publication. Since then there have been some significant changes in information about Jupiter Hammon and his family. Most importantly, two newly discovered poems have come to light recently. In 2011, Julie McCown, a student of Dr. Cedric May of Texas University, discovered at Yale University Library a poem called, "An Essay on Slavery." In 2015, independent scholar Claire Bellerjeau found another poem, "Sickness, Death, and Funeral" in the Klingenstein Library of the New

York Historical Society. This new edition, entitled "America's First Black Poet; Jupiter Hammon of Long Island," provides much new information about Hammon and will include the newly discovered poems in a larger context of the Revolutionary War and its effect.

After the finding of "Essay on Slavery," I contacted Dr. Cedric May and sent him a copy of my 1983 book on Jupiter Hammon. In 2017, Dr. May published "The Collected Works of Jupiter Hammon; Poems and Essays," by the University of Tennessee Press. Dr. May examines each of Jupiter Hammon's poems in great detail. My book contains all of Jupiter's works, but examines the larger life of Jupiter Hammon and explores his education, his life as a slave to the Lloyd Family of Long Island, and the background which resulted in his being able to produce his religious poetry. I include information on several authors who have proposed the ways in which Jupiter was able to conceal his true feelings about slavery, using codes and other means to deceive the casual reader. As the first Black Poet to publish his own verse, Jupiter was very interested in the works of Phillis Wheatley, the first female Black Poet to publish her own works, and he dedicates his poem "Address to Miss Phillis Wheatley" to her. I have included two musical compositions which will help to promote the recognition of each of them. My final emphasis is on the recognition of the work of Black poets past, present and future. I am promoting the national annual celebration of Jupiter's birthday on October 17th as Black Poetry Day, which I originated in 1970, with the purpose of recognizing the contributions which Black poets have made and are making to American life and culture.

Other new information comes from Mac Griswold's 2013 book on Shelter Island, NY. Entitled "The Manor, Three Centuries at a Slave Plantation on Long Island," her book stressed the importance of Shelter Island as a provisioning station for the Caribbean sugar plantation on Barbados Island run by several partners. It also revealed the connection of Shelter Island to the Lloyd Family of Lloyd Neck, NY through one of the partners.

"The Migration of Jupiter Hammon and His Family, From Slavery to Freedom..." by Charla E. Bolton and Rex Metcalf, appearing in the "Long Island History Journal," Volume 23 (2) 2013, gave us much information about Jupiter and his family including details of his manumission in 1795, when he was 84, and his move to Huntington Village with his grandson, Benjamin Hammon and Benjamin's wife, Phoebe. This was new information, indeed!

Searching for information on Jupiter Hammon from 1965-1970, I contacted major US collections or libraries with Black literature, several being on Long Island, New York City and in Hartford, CT. There are still possibilities that other poems and writings exist, such as in Stamford, CT. St. John's Anglican Church there received a set of divinity books by Henry Lloyd in 1790 and among the 305 listed in Kenneth Cameron's "An Anglican Library in Colonial New England," was No. 135: "Hammon, Jupiter: A gathering of his selected discourses. Unidentifiable. 'Missing in 1881,'" and many other works that presumably were "borrowed" by clergy of the day, and not returned. This happened in many early library collections. I contacted the churches, libraries and individuals in Stamford and in New Brunswick, Canada but found no trace of the missing "gathering of his selected discourses."

Since the first publication of this work in 1970, a number of events have occurred which relate to Jupiter Hammon and his poetry. On September 19, 1972, a Certificate of Commendation was awarded by the American Association of State and Local History to "American's First Negro Poet: the Complete Writings of Jupiter Hammon of Long Island ," thus recognizing both the work and the poet.

It has taken over 200 years for full recognition to be given to Jupiter Hammon, but in 1977 and in 2016 he received further acclaim. In the Congressional Record of the House of Representatives, Washington, DC, on Monday, June 20, 1977, Vol. 123 No. 106, tribute was paid by Congressman Jerome A. Ambro of Long Island.

In the Congressional Record of the House of Representatives, Washington, DC, on Monday, September 26, 2016, Vol. 162, No. 145, Congresswoman Elise Stefanik of Willsboro, NY in upstate New York, "rose to honor and recognize Black Poetry Day, which is celebrated on October 17th. While not officially recognized as a holiday, the State University of New York at Plattsburgh recognizes Black Poetry Day each year with a ceremony and a guest speaker. This event gives credence to the hard work and dedication of African Americans who have overcome adversity to express themselves through poetry. Thank you SUNY Plattsburgh for your commitment to honoring this day." Plattsburgh State University has been holding Black Poetry Readings for 35 years.

On June 25, 1977, the Association for the Study of Afro-American Life and History, 1401 14th Street N.W., Washington, DC, with Dr. J. Rupert Picott, Executive Director, honored Hammon by presenting their National Historic Marker in his name to the Lloyd Harbor Historical Society to be placed on the Lloyd Manor 1711 Salt Box House.

There are two Lloyd Manor Houses on Lloyd Neck. The first is the 1711 Henry Lloyd Manor Salt Box House, which had been thought burned, when a charred kitchen chimney lintel beam was found. Lloyd Harbor resident and Village Historian Mrs. Gordon (Lois) Holcomb, who was employed by the Huntington Public Library as Head of the Cataloging and Technical Processing Department, with Carl Anderson, a photographer friend, were recording Lloyd Harbor historic houses around 1966. They came upon the so-called "Gate House" of the Marshall Field Estate, now the property of the State of New York, and noticed a large raised panel in the front hall similar to the one in the Joseph Lloyd 1766 Manor House. She found this house was in the exact spot as the Henry Lloyd House appearing on a 1722 map of Lloyd Neck! This house was scheduled to be demolished, but her quick work and promotion of the house enabled it to be saved, restored and presented to the Lloyd Harbor Historical Society. It is now on the National Register of Historic Places. This 1711 Henry Lloyd Manor House is where Jupiter Hammon was born on October 17, 1711[*] and where he lived in his earlier years. The first owner

---

[*] Cf. Jean B. Osann. Henry Lloyd's salt Box Manor House, Huntington, N.Y., courtesy of Lloyd Harbor Historical Society, c1978, Revised Edition, c1982. 108 p.

of Jupiter Hammon was Henry Lloyd, followed by Joseph Lloyd and later, Joseph's grandson, John Lloyd II.

The second Henry Lloyd Manor House was built in 1766 by Joseph Lloyd and is now part of the Caumsett State Park and under the jurisdiction of the Long Island State Park Commission and the Office of Parks and Recreation of the State of New York. It has been placed on the National Register of Historic Places. This house is also associated with Jupiter Hammon's later years.

The complete extant writings of Hammon appear in this volume in addition to Oscar Wegelin's early contribution to the body of knowledge about him, "Jupiter Hammon: American Negro Poet," first published in 1915, and the "Critical Analysis of the Works of Jupiter Hammon," by Vernon Loggins.

Jupiter Hammon, who was born a slave in the Lloyd family, manumitted in 1795, and died in 1805, deserves to be recognized for his contribution to early Afro-American culture. His poetry is sincere and enthusiastic, and is primarily religious. Hammon's poetry reflects his great intellectual and emotional involvement with religion, to the point where it approached intoxication. It would seem likely that he was strongly affected by the renaissance of religious fervor which swept Long Island in the 1740's and 1760's, for he expresses the deep evangelical feelings of the time. Yet the medium and the form of expression, while owing much to the poetic forms of the hymn writers, is his own, with stirring similarities to Negro spirituals and to other religious folk poetry. So intent is he upon his Christian message that the words and expressions are forced into verse mold almost as a procrustean endeavor.

His later prose unquestionably served the cause of freedom, for it pictures a Heaven in which white and black are equal and are judged alike. The spiritual equality of slave and master are strongly set forth in his "Address to the Negroes in the State of New-York." He says, "The same God will judge both them and us," and "He will bring us all, rich and poor, white and black, to his judgment seat."

It is not surprising that this address, which must have dealt a blow to whites expounding a system of slavery based on a belief in racial superiority, was reprinted in 1787 by the Pennsylvania Society for Promoting the Abolition of Slavery.

Just before the publication of my first book in 1970, the exact date of Jupiter's birth was discovered by Mrs. Lillian Koppel, a graduate student in the American Studies class of Professor Louis Lomax of Hofstra University. In the back of the Lloyd ledger in the archives of the Long Island Historical Society, in Henry Lloyd's handwriting, appears a list of birth dates of his slaves, including Jupiter's as October 17, 1711.

Jupiter's works were usually found in broadsides. Until 2011, no example of his handwriting had been found except for his inscription, in a clear and bold hand, at the beginning of "A Winter Piece," on a copy in the Library of the Connecticut Historical Society in Hartford, Connecticut: "For the Rev'd William Lockwood, from His firend (sic) & humble Serv't, The Author." (The Rev. William Lockwood (1753-1828) was a Connecticut minister, installed as pastor of the First Church of Glastonbury, Connecticut, in 1797.) See copy of this example at end photos. We now have copies in Jupiter's hand of the "Essay on Slavery," of 1786. The copy of "Sickness, Death, and Funeral" of 1770 is in the hand of Phebe Townsend of Oyster Bay, NY.

Following the publication of this book in 1970, I proposed that Jupiter Hammon's birthday, October 17th, be designated as Black Poetry Day. On October 17th, 1970, the first Black Poetry Day celebration was held in the Huntington Public Library, under the sponsorship of the seven independent public libraries in the Township. Jerome A. Ambro, then Supervisor of Huntington township, issued the first proclamation designating October 17th as Black Poetry Day.

The purpose of Black Poetry Day is "to recognize the contribution of Black poets to American life and culture and to honor Jupiter Hammon, first Black in America to publish his own verse."

Notice of this event has appeared in "Chases' Calendar of Events; The Day-By-Day Directory to Special Days, Weeks and Months," published by Contemporary Books, Chicago, Illinois, which has been used by the media, schools, colleges, libraries and military bases everywhere to celebrate Black poets and Black poetry.

As a special chapter in this book, I have included an adaptation of an article I wrote for public libraries, entitled "Celebrate Black Poetry Day!" This appeared in "Bridging Cultures; Ethnic Services in the Libraries of New York State," edited by Irina A. Kuharets, Brigid A. Cahalan, and Fred J. Gitner, and published by the Ethnic Services Round Table of the New York Library Association in 2001, Albany, NY.

On June 15, 2016, a request for a Proclamation designating October 17th as Black Poetry Day in America, together with a suggested wording was sent to President Barack Obama, backed by a petition of 54 names of those attending the Black Poetry Day program signed the previous October at Plattsburgh State University College of Plattsburgh, NY. This program was planned by the PSUC Black Poetry Day Committee of Dr. Alexis Levitin, Dr. Tracie Church Guzzio, and Stanley A. Ransom, the 32nd year of celebrating this event at Plattsburgh State University. No action was taken by President Obama before his term ended.

In 1985 the State of Oregon officially passed a bill making October 17th "Black Poetry Day in Oregon," the first state to adopt this observance officially.

Black writers have always noted the special significance of poetry to African American life and culture. Nikki Giovanni said, "Poetry is part of the strong tradition of Black people." According to Julius Lester, "Poetry is the major expression of Black experience." It is my hope that our nation will continue to recognize October 17th as Black Poetry Day and to plan appropriate observances in our institutions, our schools and our libraries. Each of us can respond to the emotions and the ideas generated by Black poetry, and this should lead to a better understanding of African American life and culture.

A note about the earlier titles of my book. When they were first published, the term "Negro" was the most accepted term. This book's title has been changed to "America's First Black Poet; Jupiter Hammon of Long Island."

CHAPTER 2

JUPITER HAMMON: THE BEGINNINGS

LIKE THE WILL-OF-THE wisp that darts here and there in the darkening swamp, so snippets of information about Jupiter Hammon pop up here and there, some to continue to burn with a bright flame, others to recede as this information proves to be fanciful or unproven. the beginnings of his story, as outlined in the fascinating account by Mac Griswold, entitled "The Manor; Three Centuries as a Slave Plantation on Long Island," begins with Nathaniel Sylvester, born around 1620 in Amsterdam, "when the city reigned as Europe's center of wealth, culture and trade."[*]

His parents, Giles and Mary Arnold Sylvester, being Separatists, a dissident Protestant sect, had moved from England to the Netherlands to escape religious persecution in 1596. In Amsterdam the Sylvester's became Quakers and merchants, and started making Atlantic trips, beginning with a load of Virginia tobacco purchased from a Dutch trader in 1626. Nathaniel and his brother, Constant Sylvester, both fluent in Dutch, developed a seagoing trade with the Americas. In the first half of the seventeenth century the colonies and the Virginia coast were the focus of a swell of international trade carrying all sorts

---

[*] Griswold, Mac. The Manor; Three Centuries of a Slave Plantation on Long Island. April, 2014, c2013. Picador, NY, NY. 461p.

of European products, such as muskets and copper pots, shoes and wine, and to return carrying tobacco, beaver pelts, cotton and indigo. The Sylvester's regularly tried to outwit the Dutch revenue collectors, as did every other merchant. As products like large barrels of Virginia tobacco were hurriedly unloaded from the ships, they were followed by Amsterdam revenue agents demanding payment for duties.

Since 1639, Giles Sylvester had been directly involved with trade from the island of Barbados in the West Indies. The island produce had changed from the growing of cotton and tobacco to the harvesting of sugar cane with a labor force of enslaved Africans. The Sylvester family had changed to the production of sugar by 1646, when Constant purchased plantations and a shipping warehouse on the waterfront. Nathaniel and Constant Sylvester, Thomas Middleton and Thomas Rouse formed a partnership to develop their sugar production. The island of 166 square miles, including Constant Plantation, still produces sugar today. During the mid 1600's the partners became involved with slavery. As a source of food and provisioning, the partners purchased Shelter Island, an island of 8,000 acres, situated between the eastern forks of Long Island, for 1600 pounds of "good, merchantable Muscovado (brown) sugar," and placed Nathaniel on it to develop it. The two Sylvester brothers were attracted to Shelter Island because of its large forest of white oak timber, which was superior for making sugar hogsheads in Barbadoes.

Slaves were imported in growing numbers, since with their harsh treatment the slaves on Barbados died faster than they could reproduce. By 1642 a total of 56,800 Africans had been imported. Slaves worked on a 24 hour a day schedule, six days a week, since cut sugar cane had to be harvested and pressed quickly before it dried. By 1665, Barbados was exporting more than 15,000 tons of sugar per year.

There was always the threat of a slave uprising. By the 1690's the population of whites numbered 18,000 to 49,000 enslaved Africans and native islanders. During the summer of 1646, Nathaniel and their ninety foot ship, "Seerobbe," ventured to Guinea, Africa to pick up to

150 more slaves. Nathaniel had become both a Quaker and a man who owned slaves.

Nathaniel harvested crops and also purchased casks of meat, grain and other produce from New York and New England and sent all these provisions south from Shelter Island to Barbados to feed the slaves and the owners.

Constant shipped sugar, molasses, rum and ginger to Amsterdam, New England and England in what came to be called the "triangular trade," since items grown were exchanged for wine and manufactured goods which came from Europe or New England.

In 1653, Nathaniel married Grizzell Brinley, daughter of Thomas Brinley, one of the auditors of King Charles I. They settled into a life on Shelter Island as Quakers. At this time Quakers were being persecuted in New England. The Sylvester's offered a place where Quakers could live and be protected, and many fled to Shelter Island.

The Dutch East India Company in the 1630's had begun to import slaves to New Netherlands. A number of free Blacks and mulattoes lived in New York under Dutch rule and continued to flourish there. In 1664, Great Britain conquered New Netherlands, converting New Amsterdam to New York City and requiring residents and Long Islanders to swear allegiance to the King. By 1698 Suffolk County's census listed 558 Blacks in a total population of 2,679, about 20 percent. According to Mac Griswold, Long Islanders owned half the slaves in New York Colony.

Shelter Island had been owned in common by the four partners since 1651. Ownership and owners changed over the years as some partners sold their shares, until near the end of the seventeenth century, Nathaniel Sylvester, who had started out as the junior partner, now found that he was the sole owner of Shelter Island. Negro slaves were brought from Barbados to work on growing crops and other duties and numbered 24 slaves, the largest group of slaves in New York. Two slaves, Tamero and Oyo, had come from Nigeria and were the parents of four children, including one son, Obium, who was sold to a Boston owner, escaped and was caught, and was moved to Lloyd

Neck, Long Island. He and his wife Rose were the parents of Jupiter Hammon, born in 1711.

The Puritans of Massachusetts saw Quakers as "dangerous subversives," intent on spreading their seditious beliefs. This fear led to repressive legislation. In October, 1656 Massachusetts enacted its first anti-Quaker laws, with draconian punishments as well as heavy fines. They denounced Quaker meetings as savage and uncivilized. The Puritans were concerned at the growing number of Quaker converts who enjoyed the freedom of Quaker life and utilized civil disobedience. The Puritans also feared the Quakers because they preached in "beautiful language." Nathaniel's contribution was to create in Shelter Island a lawful sanctuary for Quakers. He claimed that earlier purchases of the Island were done independently, which removed it from government control. In 1666 Governor Richard Nicolls of New York bestowed the manor patent, confirming its independence from regional government.

The Puritans hanged many Quakers, including Mary Dyer, in Boston. Quakers appealed to King Charles II, who sent a royal writ to Governor John Endicott to prevent further executions, thus protecting the Quakers. By 1680, Puritan rule had ended.

Indian uprisings had begun in the early 1600's culminating in the destruction of the Pequot villages in Connecticut. In 1675 came another confrontation, King Philip's War, a confederacy of Algonquians who burned ninety English communities in New England. Less than a thousand colonists were killed, but at least two thousand Indians were killed in battle or executed.

Dutch troops attacked and retook New Netherlands in 1673. In 1674 Dutch troops landed at Shelter Island and ransacked storehouses and the manor house. Nathaniel had to pay the troops 500 pounds to spare his family and possessions from future damage. He also received help from Connecticut's Governor John Winthrop, whose son's warship traded shots with the Dutch troops. In March, 1674 at the Treaty of Westminster, the Dutch gave up their claim to New York Colony, which ended the Dutch empire in North America.

Nathaniel and Grizzell remained Quakers, but their children did not. Their eldest daughter, Grizzell was betrothed to Latimer Sampson, the son of an English Quaker. He died after willing all his property to Grizzell, and she later married an Anglican, James Lloyd of Boston. One part of her legacy was Lloyd Manor in Oyster Bay, Long Island. Most of the children converted to the Anglican faith.

Nathaniel died in 1680 and Grizzell died in 1687, and the Shelter Island property was inherited by their son, Giles and his four brothers, who lacked their father's business ability. By 1700 the brothers had begun to sell off the land, with Derings, Gardiners, Horsfords, and Fiskes, Sylvester descendants, owning parts of it from time to time. In 1908 the manor house was renovated and enlarged. In 1949 the property was passed to Andrew Fiske (1909-1992) and his wife, Alice Hench Fiske (1917-2006).

On a personal note, about 1965, as Director of the Huntington Public Library, a Co-Central Library of the Suffolk Cooperative Library System, I attended a meeting of the SCLS System Board of Trustees to make my report. This time the location was the Sylvester Manor House, home of Andrew and Alice Fiske. Andrew Fiske was a descendant of the earliest Sylvester owners and a member of the SCLS Board of Trustees. I drove out to the ferry and then on to Shelter Island. Following directions, I went between two stone pillars and up a long drive past an old pirate cannon to the Manor House.

Sylvestor Manor was a huge home with a long hall. I recognized not one but seven valuable Connecticut highboys lined up along the hallway. Mr. Fiske showed me an original bill of sale from the 1700's in one of the drawers. He gave us all a short history of the Manor and the Island. He also showed us the original framed patent signed by King Charles II to Nathaniel Sylvestor, hanging behind a door in the hall. It was an impressive sight.

After 2007, when Andrew Fiske's nephew, Eben Ostby took possession, he formed a 501(c)3 nonprofit corporation, Sylvester Manor Educational Farm, Inc. which will sell agricultural products and preserve the manor's heritage.

According to Dr. George Loveridge Bowen, author of books on the Lloyd family, many of the early Lloyds were physicians to the British Royal Family, starting with Queen Elizabeth I. Later, James Lloyd I came to New England in 1670 and was a merchant in Rhode Island. He met the Sylvester family of Shelter Island. Nathaniel Sylvester's daughter, Grizzel Sylvester of Shelter Island, inherited Horse Neck and married James Lloyd I in 1676. In 1677 James received a patent for Horse Neck from the British Colonial Governor, Sir Edmund Andros. In 1685 he received a Memorial Grant from King James II who added that the property shall be called "the lordship and Manor of Queens Village. When James Lloyd died in 1693, his second son, Henry Lloyd I, became the owner of the Manor of Queens Village in 1709. The property was farmed by tenant farmers.

Henry Lloyd I, 24 years old, was owner of a prosperous shipping business in Newport, Rhode Island. Upon the death of his father, he married Rebecca Nelson in Boston in 1708 and they moved to Queens Village in 1711 to develop the farm and increase its profitibility, bringing with them six slaves from Boston and a quantity of trading goods. The slaves had originally come from Shelter Island and had previously worked in the sugar plantations of Barbadoes Island. Among them were Tamero and Oyo, Negro slaves originally from Nigeria, who were the parents of four children. One son, Obium, married a slave named Rose. They were the parents of Jupiter Hammon, born October 17, 1711, and Obediah, born in 1715.

The first thing Henry Lloyd I did on moving to the Neck was to build a salt box type house in 1711 with a sloping roof rear extension. Henry had brought a large stock of Bibles, needles, trade goods and other merchandise and opened a store. He also built barns, granaries, workshops and lumberyards. A schoolhouse was later built for his children and Jupiter Hammon, the only slave to be educated. Nehemiah Bull, a 1723 Yale graduate and later minister, taught there in 1723-1724. This gave Jupiter the ability to read and to conduct activities for the Lloyd's. It is possible one of Jupiter's jobs was to mind the store and take care of some parts of business for the Lloyd family, since he was the only one who was in residence and could do it. The other slaves were rented out to local farmers or took care of other parts of the property. The Lloyds were often away on business and on the activities of a growing property with lumbering, raising of sheep and other animals and especially the growing of trees. They planted a bushel of English oak acorns which became a huge forest of oak trees. Their large stands of tall oak and chestnut trees were in great demand for ship masts in England and the colonies. The Lloyds also grew many orchards of pear and apple trees, of which the latter provided a flourishing apple cider business for the New England colonies.

During the Revolutionary War many of the Lloyds were British sympathizers, and so kept their property when the British Army occupied all of Long Island. A British fort, Fort Franklin, was built in the northern part of the Neck, named not for Benjamin Franklin, a patriot, but for Benjamin's son, William Franklin, who supported the British cause.

In 1766 and 1767 a new and larger house was built by son Joseph Lloyd at some distance from the 1711 house. It featured in the second floor a special trap door, leading to the basement and to a tunnel which exited down at the shore line. When the Revolutionary War ended in 1783, twelve British soldiers were able to escape the wrath of outside patriots by using the trap door and tunnel to escape to waiting ships. This trap door disappeared during subsequent remodeling, but I was able to take a photo of it before it disappeared, which is shown further along with a photo of the 1766 house. When patriot Joseph Lloyd escaped to Hartford, Connecticut, he took his family and slaves, including Jupiter, to Hartford, where Jupiter published several of his poems. Unfortunately, Joseph Lloyd suffered from mental depression. Hearing that the British had taken Charleston, and fearing that the patriot cause was lost, he took his own life. Jupiter Hammon then went back to Long Island as the slave of Joseph's brother. He also traveled from Hartford to New Haven to visit and assist members of the Lloyd family there, when the British attacked New Haven residents.

CHAPTER 3

JUPITER HAMMON AT THE MANOR OF QUEEN'S VILLAGE

MUCH OF THIS information comes from the detailed account of Jupiter Hammon and his family, based on extensive research by Charla E. Bolton, AICP and Reginald H. Metcalf, Jr. "The Migration of Jupiter Hammon and His Family: From Slavery to Freedom and its Consequences," was published in the Long Island History Journal, Volume 23, Issue 2, 2013.

Tamero and Oyo, from Nigeria, came separately to the Constant Sugar Plantation in Barbados in the 1660s. They and other slaves were transferred to Shelter Island, managed by Nathaniel Sylvester, to assist in preparing the shipment of provisions and goods to Barbados to maintain the slaves and owners of the sugar plantation. Their four children included Obium (c. 1668-1757). Obium was sold to James Lloyd and his wife, Grizzell in Boston in 1687. He attempted to escape, but was caught and returned. After James' death in 1693, Henry Lloyd moved from Boston to Lloyd Manor, taking with him five African slaves, Rose, Obium, Jack, Nero and Bridget. Obium and Rose had two children, Jupiter (October 17, 1711 to 1805) and Obediah (c.1715 to about 1755).

According to Dr. George Bowen, Henry brought a large stock of merchandise to the Manor and immediately opened a store. His compound consisted of his home, store, barns, granaries, workshops with looms for weaving, and lumberyards.

On December 31, 1714, when Jupiter was three years old, according to George Bowen, author of "James Lloyd II, M.D.," there is an entry in the ledgers of Henry Lloyd I for a pair of shoes for Jupiter at a cost of three shillings. Henry Lloyd I paid James Kelsie three shillings for another pair of shoes for Jupiter in 1720, when he was nine years old. On December 6, 1720, Henry Lloyd I paid James Kelsie in Huntington three shillings for another pair of shoes for Jupiter. Shoes were normally made for slaves just before winter.

The Lloyd Family were British merchants who worked at Queen's Village on Lloyd Neck and developed their Manor in the English fashion. Dorothy C. Barck, in her Introduction to the "Papers of the Lloyd Family," stated:

"After 1711, Henry Lloyd and his successors lived with their slaves and tenants on the Manor, which as regards the necessities of life, was a self-sufficient community, raising wheat, rye, and corn; vegetables and fruits; cattle, sheep, swine, and horses. The trees on the Neck were recognized as its chief source of wealth, and cord wood and timber were cut sparingly and with care not to detract from future profits. The Lloyds were good agriculturists, actively concerned in grafting fruit trees, improving the breeds of their horses and cattle, and in conserving and enriching the soil by rotation of crops and the use of fertilizers."

Around 1750 John Lloyd wrote to his son Joseph that "a day's work is from 6am to 6pm," 12 hours. (Barck, page 794).

Later John Lloyd II obtained bushels of acorns from English oak trees, which in 1790 resulted in a forest of over 2,000 English oak trees.

As the apple trees grew, so did their extensive apple cider business, renowned in all the Coastal States and New England. Their stands of tall oaks and chestnuts furnished masts for British and Colonial vessels. Land was rented to farmers for grazing sheep and cattle, and some land was rented to tenant farmers, providing they established an additional apple or fruit orchard.

In April, 1712, Henry Lloyd purchased a sloop "Wentworth" for 217 pounds and in 1727 had a larger vessel constructed for 700 pounds, to be used to ship staves and casks to the West Indies to trade for salt and other goods.

Henry Lloyd was a supporter and promoter of the Society for the propagation of the Gospel, a British missionary organization which promoted slave literacy. Slaves who were literate could then read the Bible, a primary purpose of the Society.

Jupiter grew up in the Lloyd household and was taught to read and write along with the Lloyd children, who called him "brother Jupiter." He attended school when he was twelve. The teacher, Nehemiah Bull (1701-1740) was a Yale College graduate of 1723 and later a Congregational minister in Westfield, Massachusetts. Jupiter's schooling was successful in that he was able to create and write his religious poetry without further editing, according to Charles A. Vertanes. His publisher noted that he had a "better style than could be expected from a slave," which might have led to some doubts. Jupiter first called himself Jupiter Lloyd, but later decided on the Biblical last name of Hammon.

Margaret Brucia, in her article in the "International Journal of the Classical Tradition," page 521, suggests that Henry Lloyd's inspiration for naming his slave came directly from his copy of Ogilby's Commentary in his "Aeneid," which mentions Jupiter Hammon. But Jupiter seems to have chosen his own name.

According to Charla Bolton and Reginald Metcalf, Jupiter inherited his father Obium's prayer book, which was inscribed "obium Rooe [Rose] - his book. God give him grace- 1710/11." This book was later inscribed by their son as "Jupiter Lloyd his book AD 1745." Jupiter later took the name of Hammon. Bolton/Metcalf suggests that his Bible's Glossary explained that "Jupiter" signified "salvation," and that "Hammon" was defined as "preparation," indicating to Jupiter that his name reflected his belief in Salvation Preparation. In May, 1733, when Jupiter was twenty-two years old he purchased a Bible from his master and studied it faithfully. His brother Obediah also adopted a similar name, but spelled his surname Hammond.

Jupiter "was a butler and senior servant, and apparently never married or had children," according to Bolton and Metcalf. There is no record of him being hired out as other slaves were. He grew up to be a household slave and trusted servant, helping the Lloyd family in their activities and assisting them in maintaining their property.

He also maintained the orchard called "Jupiter's Orchard," which the Lloyds stocked with apple and pear and other fruit trees. The Lloyds were able merchants and did their own bookkeeping, sales and accounting. An entry for October 6, 1790 shows a receipt for 12 pounds for bond interest which Jupiter had picked up for the Lloyd Family in Oyster Bay.

Yet, on November 17, 1750, according to the "Papers of the Lloyd Family," by Barck, on p. 471 Nathaniel Lloyd wrote to Henry Lloyd at Boston, "Jupiter, I conclude, has as much of my money in his hands, or can get it for you in a few days."

The African American educator and writer, J. Saunders Redding, in his 1939 book, "To Make a Poet Black," discusses Hammon: "Hammon was an intelligent and privileged slave, respected by the master class for his skill with tools and by the slaves for his power as a preacher." He also states, "Hammon's life was motivated by the compulsion of obedience to his earthly and his heavenly master."

The slaves usually accompanied their owners to church. Henry Lloyd was Anglican and often sailed or was rowed across Long Island Sound in his schooner "Wentworth" to attend the Episcopal Church in Stamford, Connecticut, where another Lloyd family member was living.

Henry Lloyd was permitted to obtain use of a pew at the Old First Presbyterian Church in Huntington Village, but was warned "not to ever think of bringing an Episcopal priest to this church!" Prompted by the Reverend Ebenezer Prime's sermon on the "evils of worldly wealth," to which Henry Lloyd took offense, Henry Lloyd was instrumental in establishing St. John's Episcopal Church in Huntington and also the St. John's Episcopal Church in Cold Spring Harbor nearby. About 1790, he gave his 250 volume library of religious books to the St. John's Episcopal Church in Stamford, CT. These books had been available for Jupiter to read as he was growing up. Jupiter Hammon's "dissertations and writings" were among the collection of books and religious printings listed, but these were later inventoried as "missing in 1881," and further searches have been unsuccessful. I have tracked the libraries of Dr. Dibblee, the Anglican pastor, and the library of Dr. Frederick Dibblee, his son, who ministered to the New Brunswick, Canada parishioners, but had no success in finding the lost writings of Jupiter. Perhaps they will be found in an attic in Stamford, CT.

Obediah Hammond (1715-1755) joined the St. John's Episcopal Church of Huntington and had a wife and three children, Richard (1740-90), Cato (1742-1790) and Ruth (1744-May 5, 1817). All Hammon family descendants come from Richard, Ruth and Obediah. There are descendants now still living in Huntington.

Henry Lloyd was married to a widow, Mrs. Mary Pemberton, about 1729. She was intensely religious and prayed constantly. She died in 1749, age 68. She is remembered by her son, Ebenezer Pemberton, who published her "Meditations on Divine Subjects," in 1750. She took care of the Lloyd children and would have been an influence on Jupiter Hammon, who was also much occupied with reading the Bible and other religious works. He was allowed to use the library of Lloyd Manor House. Works of Burkitt and Bishop Beverage, great divines alluded to by Hammon, are known to have been part of the library of Henry Lloyd. He also read and mentioned the works of Reverend Solomon Stoddard, pastor of the Northhampton, MA church for 60 years. (Disclosure: Reverend Stoddard was my 7th Great Grandfather and the first Librarian of Harvard College in 1666-1669.)

During Jupiter's lifetime several religious awakenings took place, which may have influenced Jupiter, who traveled widely on Long Island. The first one in 1741 swept through Long Island, stimulated by Reverend George Whitefield, George Fox and other Quaker preachers who also visited Shelter Island. The second occurred in 1763, just after Jupiter had published his "An Evenings Thought" in 1760. According to the Reverend Samuel Buell of Sag Harbor, ("A Faithful Narrative of the Remarkable Revival of Religion in the Congregation of EastHampton, on Long-Island, in the year of our Lord, 1764"), so intense was the religious fervor of the congregations that they insisted that ministers preach all day long on Sundays, even though their voices were giving out. Crowds demanded to be saved and trembled at the thought of their sins, calling on the preachers to save them from Hell.

Jupiter Hammon was able to travel, both on his master's business and on his own. He says that "he was able to do almost any kind of business." Langston Hughes states, "Hammon was an intelligent and privileged slave, respected by his master for his skill with tools and by his fellow slaves for his power as a preacher." He traveled to Philadelphia to address the Society for the Preservation of the Gospel, to which Henry Lloyd was a promoter and contributor. He also traveled to New York City to address the black populations. He may have been able to attend some of the dramatic gatherings of the Great Awakenings, which could have stimulated his desire to create religious poetry.

One unusual involvement with the Lloyd Family was their establishment of "Jupiter's Orchard." Lloyd Neck had four orchards, one large one by the bay and three smaller ones on the periphery of the Neck, as shown in the map of Queen's Village from the biography of James Lloyd II. One of these was called "Jupiter's Orchard" in many of the letters of the Lloyd Family but not on the Lloyd Neck maps. On June 4, 1773, Lloyd letters discussed "planting fruit trees adjoining Jupiter's Orchard." Henry notes, page 746, "when I plant Jupiter's Orchard, it shall be fenced." Letter from Henry Lloyd II to John Lloyd II.

Charles A. Vertanes, author of the article, "Jupiter Hammon; Early

Negro Poet of L. I.," in *The Nassau County Historical Journal,* Volume 18, No. 1, Winter, 1957, pages 1-17, suggests on page 7, "In the papers of the Lloyd family there are at least two references to 'Jupiter's Orchard.' What else could these references mean but that Jupiter Hammon was hired to himself, to work for part or all of his time as a slave-tenant in the orchard bearing his name?"

Henry Lloyd's record of apple and other trees in a Memo of 1718 includes the plantings of "rows of pairmains, Newtown pairmains, Newtown pippins, Rand apples, rupitains, rows of Queen apples, Rock apples, 'great grandmother apples,' large Green apples, Huntington Sweetings, Poltons, Pippins, and trees from Smithtown and there abouts." Fruit trees also included pear and peach trees. Maintenance of fruit trees was a problem, and fruit tree trunks were annually covered with tar to prevent canker. Fruit trees were an important product. Tenants were required to plant orchards of two acres. On September 13, 1773 Henry writes, "Please send my memorandum of fruit trees to Captain Smith and desire him to procure and send them from New York."

The source of many of the fruit trees was the 80 acre Linnaean Botanic Garden and Nurseries established at Flushing Landing, NY in 1737 by Robert Prince and his son William. Henry Lloyd referred to purchasing their fruit trees several times. The Prince's imported plants from Europe and sent American plants abroad. They also grafted new species of fruit trees and roses. George Washington and Thomas Jefferson were also purchasers of their fruit trees.

On page 863, he notes, "Put two bushels of shells around each apple tree in the young orchard." Many fruit trees were destroyed or not maintained during the Revolutionary War, when the British occupied all of Long Island and cut thousands of cords of wood of any kind for fuel. After the War, the fruit trees were again well maintained.

During the Revolutionary War the British constructed Fort Franklin at the northeastern end of Lloyd's Neck, named for Benjamin Franklin's Tory son, William Franklin. Patriot raiders came over from Connecticut from time to time to harass the fort's occupants. Legend has it that at the end of the war, British soldiers living at the Lloyd Manor were said to have escaped the wrath of local patriots by entering a secret upstairs room and creeping down through a secret passageway and through a tunnel to the harbor and the safety of their ships. My photo of the open trapdoor leading to the tunnel, now blocked, is included in the photo section of this book.

Henry Lloyd died in 1763 and the Lloyd Manor was equally divided in 1764 between his four sons and Dr. James II. Henry's will stated, "the old Negroe's near past labour, when that should happen, to be provided for in proportion." Jupiter was unusual in that his master rewarded his years of service with the proceeds from Jupiter's Orchard, which would provide him with some income in retirement. Though there are several maps in existence that show the orchards of Lloyd Neck, none of them are noted as "Jupiter's Orchard."

Under the New York law of 1785, modified in 1788, slaves were to be set at liberty. Between 1791 and 1795, Jupiter and his family and the other slaves were manumitted. Jupiter and his grandson, Benjamin Hammon, and Benjamin's wife, Phoebe, left Lloyd Manor and moved to Huntington Village, where they established new lives in the new free African American community. In 1799, when Jupiter was 88, Benjamin purchased a house from Stephen Brown for $125. Jupiter and his family's residence was at 73 West Shore Road, one of the few houses on that road about a mile north of Huntington Village. Jupiter had the income from Jupiter's Orchard, left to him by the Lloyd Family. Employment could be found in nearby mills, on sailing vessels or in local shipbuilding places. Also in the Village lived Amelia Lloyd, one of their former owners, who did provide some additional employment. A photo of the house at 73 West Shore Road is at the frontispiece.

Robert G. Hughes, Huntington Town Historian, kindly sent me a copy of the "73 West Shore Road Historic Designation Report" of July 29, 2014, for which I thank him. The seven page report made for Supervisor Petrone and members of the Town Board gives a map, photos of the inside and outside of the house, and details of the building.

The existing house was originally a story and a half structure with a salt box profile and a chimney on the southwest end. The house on one and a half acres was built about 1795 for Stephen Brown. Brown sold the house and lot to Benjamin and Phoebe Hammon in 1799 for $125.00 paid in cash. It was thus fairly new when Jupiter and his family moved in in 1799. This is also the earliest known record of land in Huntington being purchased by an African American. Jupiter Hammon was listed as head of the family in the 1800 census. The chestnut flooring and framing on the first floor are almost completely intact. Interior photos show large rooms with overhead heavy beams. The end room has a large stone fireplace and outside chimney. There is a large front porch with several columns. The house at 73 West Shore Road has now been designated an historic landmark.

According to Bolton and Metcalf's account, on January 9, 1797, Jupiter purchased rum and a jug from the store of Peleg Wood, noted in his Ledger number 4.

When Jupiter died in 1805, aged 94, his orchard income ceased, and the family was forced to apply to the town for public assistance. Jupiter's date of death and burial place have not yet been found.

Obediah's descendants continued to live in Huntington Village. I believe that one of them, Howard Johnson, lived with his family on Woodbury Road. In 1958 he became the custodian at the newly opened Huntington Public Library building at 228 Main Street, where I was the Library Director for 17 years. Unfortunately, a fire destroyed the family papers in his attic before they could be examined.

CHAPTER 4

THE WRITINGS OF JUPITER HAMMON

"A poet's pleasure is to withhold a little of his meaning,
to intensify by mystification."
In "The Practical Cogitator; or the Thinker's Anthology,"
3rd edition, Charles P. Curtis, Editor, Boston,
Houghton Miflin Co., page 529.

THE COMPLETE EXTANT writings of Hammon appear in this volume. In my previous book on Jupiter Hammon, "America's First Negro Poet," I included Oscar Wegelin's lasting contribution to the body of knowledge about him, *Jupiter Hammon: American Negro Poet.* Few persons have had an opportunity to examine Wegelin's work, issued as it was in a special limited edition in 1915, and Wegelin's study is among the few authorities on this Black poet of Long Island. He was the first writer to establish Jupiter Hammon as the first Black poet to publish his own verse, and his article is provided below. How this came about is as follows:

On the front page of "The New York Amsterdam News" of Wednesday, January 22, 1930, is an article by Arthur A. Schomburg, noted African philanthropist whose large collection of African American literature is now a part of the New York Public Research

Library. He stated, "To a white German-American, Charles F. Heartman of Metuchen, NJ is due the credit of perpetuating the memory of this sable poet (Hammon). After having brought out the Phillis Wheatley memorial edition of her poems, he asked my opinion of going into the Jupiter Hammon venture as an added feature to his series of monographs. He selected Oscar Wegelin, one of America's most noted critics and bibliophiles, to prepare the monograph. Mr. Wegelin has done a most credible compilation, knowing how scarce the facts were available in this case. Mr. Heartman presented a copy of the work to the late President Theodore Roosevelt, who in turn gave him an autograph portrait with a letter that stated Jupiter Hammon was a trusted servant in the family of Lloyds, of whom his son-in law was a descendant. Heartman was complimented for his unselfish interest in the Negro race of America." The Jupiter Hammon edition was limited to 97 copies on hand-made Fabriano paper and ten copies on Japanese vellum... and is now out of print."

The Lloyd estate, located on Long Island's North Shore, occupied the peninsula of Lloyds' Neck, between Oyster Bay and Huntington, and it was also known as Queen's Village. Henry Lloyd, who rebuilt the 1711 version of the Lloyd Manor House, owned eight Negro slaves needed to maintain the considerable property and enterprises of a prosperous merchant.

Jupiter received a better education than the average slave, and he was able to use the extensive library of Lloyd Manor House. Works of Burkitt and Bishop Beverage, great divines alluded to by Hammon, are known to be part of the library of Henry Lloyd.

Jupiter's first poem was "An Evening Thought, Salvation by Christ, with Penetential Cries: Composed by Jupiter Hammon, a Negro belonging to Mr. Lloyd, of Queen's-Village, on Long-Island, the 25th of December, 1760." This 88 line poem was published as a broadside. He introduces his brethren to the subject of Salvation, which he uses some 23 times:

"Salvation comes by Jesus Christ alone
The only Son of God;
Redemption now to every one,
That love his holy Word."

One other earlier Black poet should be mentioned. Lucy Terry Prince, a slave from Deerfield, Massachusetts, wrote a poetic account of a battle which took place in 1746 between the Deerfield settlers and the Native Americans in a place called "the Bars Meadow," hence the title of her work was "Bars Fight." It was not published by her, but appeared in 1855 in Josiah Gilbert Holland's "History of Western Massachusetts."

Hammon's next poem was a poem on "Sickness, Death and Funeral," an unpublished poem dated August 10, 1770. Claire Bellerjeau, who discovered the poem in the Townsend archives in the New York Historical Society, states that the poem was not in Jupiter's hand, but was copied later by Phebe Townsend. See later on for further information about this poem.

Upon the decease of Henry Lloyd in 1763, Hammon became the property of Joseph Lloyd, an American patriot. After 1775, at the start of the Revolutionary War, the British Army overran Long Island, and sought to punish anyone who was declared a patriot. When Joseph Lloyd fled from the approaching British Army, his family and slaves accompanied him to Stamford, Connecticut, where his brother John was living, and later moved to Hartford.

Hammon's next four works were published in Hartford, then the literary capital of the Colonies. *An Address to Miss Phillis Wheatly* appeared in 1778:

"O come you pious youth! adore
The wisdom of thy God,
In bringing thee from distant shore,
To learn His holy word."

Next in 1779 was the elusive *Essay on the Ten Virgins*, published as a broadside by Hudson & Goodwin. It was advertised in the Connecticut Courant for December 14, 1779. No copy of this article has been discovered.

An Evening's Improvement. Shewing, the Necessity of beholding the Lamb of God. To which is added, A Dialogue, Entitled, The Kind Master and Dutiful Servant, was "Printed during the Revolution, probably in 1779 by Hudson & Goodwin. The first is a prose sermon to the brethren, meant to be heard, on seeking the Lord and eternal life. In the attached "Dialogue", the Servant states"

"Dear Master, now it is a time,   The Master replies: "Then will
    the happy day appear,
A time of great distress;   That virtue shall increase;
We'll follow after things divine,   Lay up the sword and drop the
    spear,
And pray for happiness."   And nations seek for peace."
An often quoted passage: "Believe me now my Christian friends
    Believe your friend call'd Hammon:
    You cannot to your God attend,
    And serve the God of Mammon."

During this time, around 1779, Jupiter traveled in Connecticut, especially to visit the Hillhouse family 40 miles away in New Haven. Sarah Lloyd had married James Townsend, a Captain in the American forces, and the family resided in New Haven. They had a difficult time during the Revolution, since the British in July, 1779 attacked New Haven and killed many of the patriots. Sarah was pregnant with her first child, and unfortunately mother and child did not survive.

Later, additional tragedy had come to the exiled Lloyd family. On June 18, 1780, Joseph Lloyd, hearing of the surrender of Charlestown, and believing it to be fact, thought the American cause was lost, and in a despondent mood took his own life. The Reverend Nathan Perkins eulogized him in "A Sermon Occasioned by the Unhappy

Death of Mr. Lloyd: a Refugee from Long Island," on July 26th, 1780 in Hartford. On page 8-9, Reverend Perkins states, "The awful death that gave occasion to this discourse and led to the above train of reflections, is a remarkable instance to what length, melancholy gloom and dejection of spirit, through the temptation of a subtle adversary, may be carried. Mr. Lloyd, who was left of God to commit the crime of suicide, was in an exile state. On the commencement of the present dispute between Great Britain and America, he chose the side of Liberty and his Country. When the enemy took possession of Ling-Island, he came over to Stamford, in Connecticut, where a brother of his lived, and left his estate on the island, which suffered much by the enemy. He was a sincere friend to his country.—A man of uncommon humanity, compassion and tenderness.—Very harmless and inoffensive, always appearing to wish the prosperity and not the hurt of his fellow-creatures.—The distress of the times and his own sufferings, preyed much upon his spirits, and sometimes threw him into despondence.—On hearing of the surrender of Charlestown, and believing it to be fact, he gave up our cause for lost, thought the country must be subdued, and that the enemy might make their own terms; he could not survive the shock The gloominess of the prospect seemed to overpower his mind, and he, to get rid of trouble, unhappily put a period to his own life." The effect upon the family must have been devastating. It was as great for Jupiter Hammon, for it meant a new master, John Lloyd, Joseph's grandson, and later at War's end, a return to the Lloyd Manor.

A Winter Piece; being a serious exhortation, with a call to the Unconverted; and a short contemplation on the death of Jesus Christ, was a prose piece published in Hartford in 1782.

It includes a reference to Reverend Solomon Stoddard, of Northhampton, Massachusetts.

"A Poem for Children with Thoughts on Death was published in Hartford, January 1, 1782.

Overton's *Long Island's Story* states that in 1782 Hammon composed a set of verses, not yet found and possibly not published, to celebrate the visit of young Prince William Henry, later King William IV, to Lloyd Manor House. This was the first visit to America by any member of the British Royal family, and the Prince, then called Duke of Clarence, "displayed a lively and democratic temperament which delighted Jupiter Hammon." However, according to "A History of the Joseph Lloyd Manor House," by Kenneth Scott and Susan E. Klaffly, SPLIA, 1976, p. 28, " the legend that Jupiter Hammon composed verses to celebrate the Prince's visit to the house is without foundation, for at that time Jupiter, following the death of Joseph Lloyd in 1780, was in Connecticut and the slave of John Lloyd II, an ardent patriot."

The Prince traveled around Long Island and also visited the nearby Fort Franklin, home to 800 Loyalists and other British forces, accompanied by its designer, Colonel Benjamin Thompson, later Count Rumford, who together with other officers from the fort were residing in Lloyd Manor House.

Incidentally, Count Rumford was notorious for his mean and savage attitude toward the Long Island patriots. Colonel Thompson, while in Huntington, had his soldiers erect a fort, called Fort Golgotha, atop the local burying ground, and used the timbers torn from the Presbyterian Church to form the walls of the Fort.

He detested Reverend Ebenezer Prime, an outspoken patriot, and he placed his tent where he was living on the burying ground so that every time he went in and out, he could, as he said, "tread on the head of the Old Rebel," who had lately died and been interred in the cemetery. He ordered his troops to knock over the marble tombstones of patriot families in Huntington graveyards and make ovens of them, so that he could show the patriots "tombstone bread," loaves of bread with their ancestor's inscriptions on them. To this day, when I was there, some of the older residents still would not purchase Rumford baking powder or other products bearing the hated name.

In 2011, Julie McCown, a graduate student of Dr. Cedric May, a University of Texas at Arlington English professor, discovered a previously unknown Hammon poem in the Hillhouse Family Papers

Manuscripts and Archives at Yale University's Sterling Memorial Library. James Hillhouse was a Yale graduate, a Revolutionary War Captain, a Connecticut lawyer, and a friend of the Lloyd family. He married Sarah Lloyd, who, as mentioned, died in childbirth. The poem is called *An Essay on Slavery, with submission to Divine providence, Knowing that God Rules over all things,* "composed by Jupiter Hammon, A Negro Man belonging to Mr. John Lloyd, Queens-Village on Long Island." It is dated November 10, 1786. Dr. May suggests it may be a draft to accompany the *Address to the Negroes of the State of New York,* which was published the next year. In *Early American Literature,* volume 48, number 2, pages 457-471, dated 2013, Dr. May offers the poem and discusses its importance and its meaning in the life of Jupiter Hammon. His excellent research also adds explanation of sections or words in the text. The Essay poem starts:

"Our forefathers came from Africa   "Dark and dismal was the Day
Tost over the raging main   When slavery began
To a Christian shore there for to stay All humble thoughts were put away
And not return again."   Then slaves were made by Man."

Dr. May issued "The Collected Works of Jupiter Hammon," in 2017, published by the University of Tennessee Press, focusing on Jupiter's Poems and Essays.

In 2015, independent scholar Claire Bellerjeau discovered a new Hammon poem in the New-York Historical Society's Patricia D. Klingenstein Library while conducting research on the slaves of the Townsend Family of Oyster Bay, NY. It had no leading title, but included three prominent attached words, "Sickness, Death, and Funeral" and calls upon "Ye youth of Boston town" to mourn the death of "a pious youth" who" Always did appear to be A chosen child of god." While it was written by Jupiter Hammon on August 10, 1770, when Phebe Townsend (1763-1841) was but seven years old, she apparently recopied the poem later on in her own mature handwriting. The next to last verse notes that "Dear Hutchinson is dead and gone and Left a Memorial." Anne Hutchinson (1591-August,1643) was an outspoken Puritan spiritual adviser who was banished from the Massachusetts Bay Colony in 1637 for avowing that a person's individual beliefs and conduct was strictly between that person and God. This threatened the Puritan ministers who objected to her preaching, especially to groups of women, and which suggested a personal salvation rather than one offered through ministers. Anne and her family moved to Long Island and later to Pelham Neck, near New Rochelle, where in 1643 she, and all but one of her children were killed by Native Americans. Jupiter was of the same mind as Anne Hutchinson. His poem celebrates the "pious youth" who speaks directly to Jesus and God.

Jupiter's last work was the aforementioned *An Address to the Negroes in the State of New York,* published in 1787, with Hammon noted as "servant of John Lloyd, jun., Esq." in Queen's Village. His later prose unquestionably served the cause of freedom, for it pictures a Heaven in which white and black are equal and are judged alike. The spiritual equality of slave and master are strongly set forth in his *Address to the Negroes in the State of New-York.* He says, "The same God will judge both them and us," and "He will bring us all, rich and poor, white and black, to his judgment seat."

It is not surprising that this address, which must have dealt a blow to whites expounding a system of slavery based on a belief in racial superiority, was reprinted in 1787 by the Pennsylvania Society for Promoting the Abolition of Slavery. In this same address Hammon delivers arguments in favor of the abolition of slavery, and he states that he "would be glad if others, especially the young Negroes, were to be free." How ironic, he writes, that slavery should exist at the same time that the white people are spending their money and losing their lives for the cause of liberty in the American Revolution! For himself, a man of over seventy, he does not wish freedom, as he would "hardly know how to take care of himself," but he acknowledges that " liberty is a great thing, and worth seeking for." He ends with an appeal to his readers, the brethren. "Let me beg of you then, ...for the sake of your poor brethren, who are still in bondage, "to lead quiet and peaceable lives in all Godliness and honesty."

For Jupiter, freedom came eight years later, and he and his family were manumitted in 1795, enabling Jupiter, his grandson Benjamin Hammon and Benjamin's wife, Phoebe to move to Huntington Village. Jupiter was able to support the family using proceeds from "Jupiter's Orchard," which the Lloyd Family offered him upon his manumission. Jupiter died in 1805, but his burial site, possibly in a graveyard behind an Episcopal or African Methodist Episcopal Church has not been located. Following Jupiter's death, the income from the Orchard stopped, jobs were scarce, and the family was forced to seek public assistance from the Town.

CHAPTER 5

WRITINGS ABOUT
JUPITER HAMMON

BIOGRAPHICAL MATERIAL ON Jupiter Hammon was very slight until "The Manor," by Mac Griswold appeared and especially the Charla Bolton/Rex Metcalf article, *The Migration of Jupiter Hammon and His Family: From Slavery to Freedom and its Consequences, Volume 23, Issue 2, 2013* in "Long Island History," which gave a detailed account of Jupiter's forebears, his birth on Lloyd Neck and later life and freedom. He was largely ignored by writers of the nineteenth century, and he was probably unknown to those writers listing the achievements of other Black writers. In contrast, the name of Phyllis Wheatley is often mentioned, perhaps due partly to her celebrated correspondence with George Washington.

To Oscar Wegelin must go the credit for discovering Jupiter Hammon and bringing him to the attention of the world. Following Emily Foster Happer's article, *The First Negro Poet of America,* in the Literary Collector of 1904 in which she nominates Phillis Wheatly for this honor, Oscar Wegelin published a reply later in the same magazine. In rebutting a statement that Phyllis Wheatley was America's first Negro poet, Wegelin introduced Jupiter Hammon in an article *Was Phillis Wheatley America's First Negro Poet?* in the *Literary Collector* for August, 1904, (p. 117-118) but lacked, at that time the necessary proof. Upon obtaining the necessary documentation, finding that a copy of Hammon's "An Evening Thought," his first published poem, was in the collections of the New York Historical Society Library, Oscar Wegelin produced his *Jupiter Hammon: American Negro Poet*, article in 1915. Wegelin thus backed up his claim and at the same time providing an extensive treatment of the Long Island slave-poet.

Wegelin's book has been the basis for most of the articles appearing in reference books and periodicals. Benjamin Brawley contributed an excellent two-column treatment of Hammon in the *Dictionary of American Biography*, and he acknowledged the Wegelin account to be the most accessible source and at that time practically the sole authority on Hammon. Brawley also considered the contribution of Hammon to Negro literature in his *Early Negro American Writers*, published in 1935. He credits Hammon's *Address to the Negroes* with helping to influence later New York State legislation to abolish slavery within the State of New York.

Critical treatment of Hammon's poetry is offered by Vernon Loggins in his *The Negro Author, His Development in America to 1900*. Loggins acknowledges Hammon's unique contribution to American poetry in the eighteenth century, calling his verse the precursor of the Negro spiritual and remarkable for its touch of originality. Loggins' appraisal of Hammon is presented later in this volume preceding Hammon's poetry.

Reverend Charles A. Vertanes offers some revealing information about Hammon in his *Jupiter Hammon, Early Long Island Poet*, appearing in the Winter, 1957 issue of the *Nassau County Historical Journal*. This seventeen page study was based upon original research in the archives of the Long Island Historical Society, which holds many unpublished papers and account books of the Lloyd family. Rev. Vertanes discusses Hammon as a religious poet and also contributes much to the understanding of the early influences upon Hammon, who may have been seeking out ways to resist slavery. This study is particularly useful in setting forth what is known about Hammon's schooling and reading. Henry Lloyd owned a fine library and had a strong desire to dispense knowledge, even importing books for sale, and he was generous in lending and in giving books to his friends and tenants. Hammon would have benefitted from such access to books and must have flourished in the intellectual atmosphere of Lloyd Manor House.

An informative history of the slavery system and the abolition movement in New York State appears in Edgar J. McManus' book, *A History of Negro Slavery in New York*, published in 1966. In the eighteenth century the arguments and attacks of missionaries and other religious leaders were very effective in halting the spread of slavery in New York State. The laws of New York State which curtailed slavery, freed some classes of slaves and which restricted the manumission of aged slaves, were passed in the 1780's, when Jupiter Hammon was in his seventies.

We know now that Jupiter, his brother Obediah, and his family were all manumitted from 1791 to 1795 and moved to Huntington Village, thanks to research done by Charla E. Bolton and Reginald H. Metcalf in their article, *The Migration of Jupiter Hammon and His Family: From Slavery to Freedom and its Consequences*, published in the Long Island History Journal, 2013, Volume 23, issue 2. This article charts Jupiter Hammon's family from the 1600's through the early 1800's. Tamero, husband of Oyo, came from the Igbo-speaking Ibo part of Nigeria, and his wife, Oyo, came from the Yoruba-speaking kingdom of Oyo. They arrived separately in the early 1660's to the Constant Plantation, owned by Constant and Nathaniel Sylvester. The Sylvesters also owned Shelter Island, between the forks of Long Island, where provisions were gathered and sent to support the Barbados owners and slaves.

Nathaniel Sylvester obtained a royal warrant establishing the Manor of Shelter Island in 1666, and subsequently moved Tamero and Oyo and their son Obium there along with other slaves needed to work the land. Tamera and Oyo died there and were buried at Sylvester Manor. Obium was later sold to James and Grizzell Sylvester Lloyd and taken to their Boston home. He attempted to escape on horseback in 1691 but was caught and returned to Boston. After James died in 1693, his brother Henry Lloyd relocated from Boston to Lloyd Neck, NY, formerly owned by Grizzell Sylvester, whose first betrothed had died and left her his ownership of Lloyd Neck. Henry also brought his slaves Obium (1668-1757) and Rose (1681-1745) to Lloyd's Neck. Obium and Rose became parents of two sons, Jupiter and Obediah.

Jupiter was born on October 17, 1711, and Obediah was born in 1715. Jupiter and Obediah and their families were manumitted between 1791 and 1795. They moved to Huntington Village and took up residence at 73 West Shore Road. Jupiter died in or about 1805. We much appreciate the good research done by Charla Bolton and by Reginald Metcalf, with whom I served in the Long Island Chapter of the Sons of the American Revolution.

Manisha Sinha has issued in 768 pages in 2016 the most extensive study of the history of abolition of slavery, starting well before Hammon's time. "The Slave's Cause; A History of Abolition," was published by Yale University Press and was the product of ten years of research. She called Hammon "an accountant in the [Lloyd's] community store," which I cannot verify. She also states, on page 31 that "Hammon emphasized the regenerating power Christianity held for enslaved Africans..." He further states, "The only safety that I see, Is Jesus' holy word." On page 47, the author states that Hammon, in addressing his critics, "makes clear that only education, not inherent racial difference, separates him from his white critics." Hammon further writes that thousands of slaves "have been born in what are called Christian families," and questions the Christianity of their enslavers. On page 80 the author notes Hammon's criticism of slaveholders' hypocrisy, in spending money and losing lives in the late war to defend their own liberty, but neglecting to set their slaves free. "Hammon acknowledged the rise of the abolition movement and asked slaves to "prevail on our masters to set us free."

One of the best accounts of the life of Jupiter Hammon can be found in Sondra A. O'Neale's *Jupiter Hammon and the Biblical*

Beginnings of African-American Literature, published in 1993 as an ATLA Monograph Series, No. 28, by the American Theological Library Association and the Scarecrow Press, Inc. of Metuchen, NJ. She discusses each of Hammon's works, with extensive notes and Biblical reasonings. O'Neale says, "A devout evangelical Christian, Hammon had been converted during the earliest stirrings of the Great Awakening. As a writer he used Christianity and its foundation of biblical language, allusion, and imagery to mount a public assault against slavery." And, "His offering included the first, and most comprehensive, statement of Black theology as well as the earliest antislavery protests by a Black writer in all of American literature.... Hammon's dual commitment to Christianity and freedom has been either undervalued or ignored." She stresses that Hammon was looking for "a metaphorical vehicle for surreptitious discussion of his own enslavement and of the slave state." "Hammon had no choice but to wage war against slavery in the biblical arena."

She also states that modern critics who would have Hammon on courage insurrection do not understand the general police state conditions for slaves in New York. During the suppression of the "Negro Plot" in New York City in 1712, of the one hundred fifty Negroes arrested, "eleven were burned, eighteen were hanged, and seventy-one transported," (e.g., sold down South). O'Neale states, "Hammon tried to keep slaves alive and out of jail."

With the growing awareness of the black contributions to American literature, there are a number of articles urging the review of American literature and the teaching of a respect for the contributions of both black and white authors. One of these which mentions Jupiter Hammon is written by an educator, Carolyn Reese, in her article, *From Jupiter Hammon to LeRoi Jones*, appearing in *Changing Education, Fall, 1966*. She sees Jupiter Hammon as the first of a long line of neglected Negro authors, and she calls upon all teachers to inform their students about the contributions of Black authors to American literature. This point of view is now becoming accepted, and many high schools and colleges offer special courses of programs in the areas of Black studies as well.

In 1973 appeared *Their Eyes on the Stars: Four Black Writers,* by Margaret Goff Clark, Garrard Publishing Company, which included *Jupiter Hammon; America's First Black Poet in Print,* a 26 page juvenile biography of Jupiter Hammon which covered his life in some detail and was an excellent introduction to Jupiter for young people.

James Lloyd II, M.D. (1728-1810) And His Family on Lloyd Neck, by George Loveridge Bowen, Privately Printer, c1988, notes facts about Jupiter and has a three page separate Appendix 3 at the end which gives more details of Jupiter's life, education and writings.

The Black Presence in the Era of the American Revolution, revised edition, by Sidney Kaplan and Emma Nogrady Kaplan, was published by the University of Massachusetts Press in 1989. Jupiter Hammon occupies pages 191-200. In it the authors discuss Jupiter's life and analyze the effect of his poetry. They suggest that part of his wider importance was that he was "a preacher to the slaves in the communities of Long Island and Connecticut, where he labored for the Lloyds." p.194. To those whites who apparently objected to his preaching the Word, Jupiter offers, "I shall endeavor by divine assistance to enlighten the minds of my brethren," and he "asks leave to enquire into the state of children in Christian families, whether the children of Christian families have been taught to read and learnt their catechism?" p. 196. Their final conclusion: "Jupiter Hammon was a genius of a sort and no time-serving hypocrite. He pursued his argument, for what it was worth, with skill and conviction... What finally remains is the sense of his titanic struggle for a position as a black and a slave in a white world that called itself Christian." p. 200.

Further information on the effect of the British Invasion is given by Charles Hervey Townshend in his 1879 book, "The British Invasion of New Haven, Connecticut, Together with some Account of Their Landing, and Burning the Towns of Fairfield, and Norwalk, July, 1779,"in which, on page 53 to 55 he details the cruel attack on the citizens of New Haven. The members of the James Hillhouse family fortunately escaped.

Sondra A. O'Neale, in her chapter, *Jupiter Hammon of Long Island: America's First Black Writer,* in *Long Island Studies: Evoking a Sense of Place,* edited by Joann P. Krieg, Heart of the Lakes Publishing, 1988, cautions modern critics to look again at the influence of the church in the eighteenth century. She writes, "America's slave system was born of contorted interpretations of Christianity... Jupiter Hammon had no choice but to wage war against slavery in the Biblical arena." She notes, p. 120, "Most current literary criticism of Jupiter Hammon's works reflects anachronistic thinking and ignores the racism pervasive in all aspects of a slave society... American critics should give artists imprisoned by slavery the greatest benefit of doubt. They should also seek hidden codes and patterns that will unlock the shackled writers' intended meaning."

This suggestion is carried out in an article by Arlen Nydam, "Numerological Tradition in the Works of Jupiter Hammon," p. 207-220, in *African American Review,* volume 40, number 2, Summer, 2006. The author suggests that Jupiter "developed a style of writing with multiple layers of meaning," first biblical but with coded subtexts. His ideas about the use of numbers "most likely came through *Paradise Lost,* Pluche's *History of the Heavens,* and other authors, such as Solomon Stoddard, which he may have borrowed. His message to his fellow slaves is to learn to read, especially the Bible, but also to read his poems to learn his coded messages. O'Neale suggests "Obviously the critic must break hidden codes and patterns to unlock the shackled writers' intended meaning." It is suggested also that Phillis Wheatley's poems were also encoded protests, and that Jupiter Hammon used the same technique in his poem addressed to her, "with a message of abolitionist subversion, veiled in the language of the Bible." Hammon used Number Symbolism, a product of Renaissance thought. "The number 23 is ubiquitous in Hammon's poetry, serving a symbolic function in each poem in which he uses it. *"An Evening Thought"* is his first poem, mentioning "salvation" 23 times. The number 23 was used by Donne and other poets as a symbol of religious conversion. According to O'Neale "In the spring of

1730, when he was about nineteen years old, Jupiter became gravely ill with a goutlike disease. Three years later he purchased a Bible from his owner Henry Lloyd. The bout of sickness along with the purchase of a Bible were typical indications of a dramatic religious conversion in the eighteenth century". Hill, Patricia Liggins, ed. *Call and Response: The Riverside Anthology of the African American Literary Tradition, Boston, Houghton, Mifflin, 1998)*. Hammon uses the number 23 in several places in his poetry. O'Neale also shows Hammon's use of the numerological subtext in his prose writing, *"Dialogue Entitled the Kind Master and the Dutiful Servant,* in which the number 23 is used as a biblical subtext connoting justice and mercy and as a symbol of God's creation and reminds him of his function to act as a light to his fellow slaves.

Phillip M. Richards explains Hammon's nationalist point of view in his "Nationalist themes in the Preaching of Jupiter Hammon." In: Early American Literature, Vol. 25, No 2, 1990, pp. 123-138. "Hammon called upon Afro-Americans to assert themselves as a nation within a nation, retaining their African identity while continuing to exist within American Society." Hammon makes "his and his audience's shared ethnic identity into the basis of a national identity." (p. 124) Hammon offers Israel as a type of the Afro-American nation and hopes their history can be "a repetition of the Israelite experience."

The best book on Jupiter's poetry is Dr. Cedric May's "The Collected Works of Jupiter Hammon; Poems and Essays," issued in 2017 by the University of Tennessee Press. Dr. May examined each of the works of Jupiter Hammon and discusses their meaning and context in great detail.

In Carlton Maybee's "Black Education in New York State; From Colonial to Modern Times," the education of Jupiter Hammon is covered on pages 12-16. Many Anglican families saw that their slaves were educated and taught to read. Jupiter, in turn, on page 12, challenges all slave masters, telling them that it is their duty to give the slave children born in their households a Christian education. "Have they been baptized, taught to read, and learnt their catechism?" he asks.

There are several books describing the history of the Lloyd Manor homes where Jupiter lived and worked. *The Lloyd Manor of Queens Village,* by the Reverend Melancthon Lloyd Woolsey, published in Baltimore, 1925, reprinted 1951 by the Society for the Preservation of Long Island Antiquities (SPLIA); *A History of the Joseph Lloyd Manor House,* by Kenneth Scott and Susan E. Klaffly, published in 1976 by SPLIA, Setauket, NY; and *Henry Lloyd's Salt Box Manor House,* by Jean B. Osann, published in 1982 (c1978) by The Lloyd Harbor Historical Society in Huntington, NY. Each contain photos, maps, some mention of Jupiter, and an account of the successive owners of the house.

While the body of writings about Jupiter Hammon is small but growing fast, with the discovery of two unpublished poems in his handwriting, there is a present awareness of the earlier neglect of Black authors and a corresponding increase in the amount of material being written about them. This current attempt to place Black poets as contributors to history and literature and not as a by-product of it will have a salutary effect on the writings of Jupiter Hammon and will help to establish his honored place in American literature. This is also the aim of Black Poetry Day, which is "to recognize the contribution of Black poets to American life and culture, and to honor Jupiter Hammon, first Black in America to publish his own verse."

Distinguished professor Russel B. Nye, in a June, 1940 article in *Long Island Forum, page 129-30,* notes that Jupiter Hammon was, "as far as can be determined, the first negro in the American colonies to write poetry, a distinction in itself, and he remains Long Island's peculiar property." Nye sees Hammon as a poet who uses rime and meter "of the simplest type, and in the tradition of the ballad, the hymnal, and his earlier Puritan predecessors." He suggests that Hammon "probably followed the example and tradition of Isaac Watt s, the Methodist hymn writer who died in 1748..."

The acceptance and promotion of October 17th as Black Poetry Day will also offer a chance to further promote the works of Black writers. While this day has been observed as Black Poetry Day since 1970, I issue a call to action to libraries, schools, colleges, community groups and military installations to herald the works of Black writers. In a separate chapter, I offer suggestions for this promotion. A Black Poetry Day Center is being established in Plattsburgh, New York, at the Plattsburgh State University College, which has officially cele-brated Black Poetry Day for 33 years by inviting noted Black poets to read and discuss their works in mid-October to audiences from 120 to 600, the latter occurring when our speaker, Derek Walcott had just received his Pulitzer Prize for Poetry.

Feeling that the variations in spelling used by Jupiter Hammon and the printer give the work more flavor and authenticity, I have cor-rected the misspellings in only three or four instances, and then solely to avoid confusion.

Stanley Austin Ransom, Jr.

CHAPTER 6

JUPITER'S LIFE: A PUZZLE

JUPITER HAMMON'S LIFE is filled with anomalies. He is born in 1711 on Lloyd Neck and was allowed to go to the Lloyd Family school to be educated by Neamiah Bull, the Harvard trained teacher. He was educated with the Lloyd children, who are not named, but their close association enables him to be addressed as "brother Jupiter." Neither his brother Obediah nor other Black slave children seem to have this relationship, nor are they mentioned as being given an education. He is never mentioned as being handicapped or disabled in any way. The second Mrs. John Lloyd, who took care of the house and the children and slaves, was very religious and wrote a book on her religious "Meditations." She may have influenced Jupiter to become more religious.

While most of the other slaves are sent to work in the fields or "bound out" or rented to local farmers, Jupiter seems to be a house servant, perhaps a "butler," as Langston Hughes states. He is sent on errands to pick up money due the Lloyds, and perhaps he helps in similar ways. He is not a bookkeeper, nor an accountant, nor is he mentioned as helping Henry and Joseph Lloyd run their businesses. He is absent from any of their business ledgers, except for the early one giving the birth dates of the eight slaves, including Jupiter. The Lloyds were able businessmen, concerned with running their plantation and taking care of their business transactions themselves. Their frequent letters are concerned with the cost of fruit trees and the sale of bushels of apples, and whether tar on fruit trees will remove the "canker." Jupiter is not mentioned in the many letters of the family members, except if he is sick or will be given an old saddle. He is not part of the extensive business activities of the Lloyd Family. The Lloyd Family seem to be proud of Jupiter and his ability to preach and have given him time to do this, perhaps to benefit his fellow slaves.

Curiously, he is given an orchard to take care of. No other family members have their own orchard. There are five orchards of at least two acres each, which can hold a considerable number of apple and pear trees. Harvesting results in having bushels of Newtown Pippins and other fruit to sell or give away to relatives. Of the five orchards, one is very large and there are four smaller ones. Though not identified in any of the maps, one of the smaller orchards is known as "Jupiter's Orchard." The Preservation Long Island curators have not been able to identify which orchard was Jupiter's. Henry Lloyd identifies purchases of fruit trees from Captain Prince from New York City for "Jupiter's Orchard." He also notes other plantings as being "near Jupiter's Orchard." Jupiter evidently sold some of his fruit, for he had money to purchase a Bible from Henry Lloyd. He has time to read the Bible.

Charles A. Vertanes, author of the article, "Jupiter Hammon; Early Negro Poet of L. I.," in The Nassau County Historical Journal, Volume 18, No. 1, Winter, 1957, pages 1-17, suggests on page 7, "In the papers of the Lloyd family there are at least two references to 'Jupiter's Orchard.' What else could these references mean but that Jupiter Hammon was hired to himself, to work for part or all of his time as a slave-tenant in the orchard bearing his name?" Perhaps that is the answer.

Why is he so favored? Why is he not used to help with the Lloyd's business? We know he is helped to publish his poems "with the help of his friends," which must include the Lloyd Family. His work as a butler? He is also allowed to travel, perhaps with members of the Lloyd Family, to give talks in New York City and in Philadelphia. Slaves in the eighteenth century were not usually allowed to travel alone. Yet he traveled to Hartford, to New York City and Philadelphia, to Raynham Hall in Oyster Bay and other places. Jupiter may have traveled around Long Island in the 1740's and 1760's to hear the famous evangelist preachers during the religious revival of those time. Some writers call him a "preacher to his people," which might go along with Henry Lloyd's strong support of the Society for the Propagation of the Faith, and their encouragement of masters teaching their slaves to read, especially the Bible.

When Jupiter went with Joseph Lloyd to Hartford, CT during the Revolutionary War, he published several poems, "helped by friends." He knew several ministers and inscribed one poem to Rev. Lockwood, and thereby gave us our first look at his writing, since we know only the published poems up to this time. Later we have the "Essay on Slavery," in Jupiter's hand. Jupiter also traveled to New Haven, a distance of about 40 miles, to see the Hillhouse Family, one of whom married a Lloyd. Jupiter would have visited the Hillhouse family at the time of the Revolutionary War when the British attacked New Haven.

The poem on "Sickness, Death, and Funeral," transcribed by Phebe Townsend, of Oyster Bay, some distance from Lloyd's Neck, was discovered in 2015 in the Klingenstein Library in the New York Historical Society by Madison, CT scholar Claire Bellerjeau. This is addressed to "the pious youth of Boston town," and is dated August 10, 1770.

Jupiter's "Essay on Slavery," discovered by Julie McCown at Yale University, is a well written 25 verse poem of several pages, and critical of slavery, done in 1786, the year before his "Address to the Negroes of the State of New-York" appeared.

Much of Jupiter's prose writings were created to be read and used by "my brethren," as he called his fellow slaves. His stated intention was to advise and council other slaves, "in order to keep them out of jail," as well as to encourage them to seek Christ as their Saviour. Jupiter's position is certainly an odd one, compared with how most of the slaves were treated during the 1700's. He was even given the income from Jupiter's Orchard when he was manumitted in 1795 which was enough to provide support for Jupiter and his brother's family and their home at 73 West Shore Road in Huntington Village. An unusual form of Social Security.

The existence of another treasure trove of Jupiter's writings has come to my attention, but, alas, it leads to a dead end. Kenneth Cameron noted in his study of the Stamford, CT Anglican Library Collection given by Henry Lloyd in 1795 that there was a collection of Jupiter Hammon's "dissertations and other works" included in the library, but they were "missing in 1881." Someone borrowed them and didn't return them to the Stamford Anglican Church Library. Are they still in Stamford, CT, somewhere? Thus Henry Lloyd I thought enough of Jupiter's writings to present a collection of his "dissertations and other works" to the Anglican Library.

Another puzzling thing is the absence of any corroborating letters, news articles, or any current descriptions of Jupiter Hammon. No one has written anything to do with him, his looks, height, color, or his speeches and sermons after these occurred. Speeches of Whitefield and other orators were detailed in the press. No reports of Jupiter's audience at his New York City and Philadelphia appearances, which were encouraged and sponsored. But nothing has been discovered to describe Jupiter, the man. Perhaps a lack of Long Island news media for 1805 is partly to blame, as we have no accounts of the day, time and circumstances of his death. His poetry was locally known.

But of the man, not a word. We are left to appreciate what we know from his writings. But of the man, the puzzle remains.

The only conclusion I come to, as set forth in Chapter 2, is based upon the earlier statement of Henry Lloyd's first appearance at Lloyd Neck. He was a merchant and his business was to make sales to gain a profit. His first action was to build a house in 1711. His second was to open a store. I conclude that Jupiter's main occupation was to maintain the store for the Lloyd family. I have noted that there was no one else who had the time and the education to accomplish this as his career, and he would have been capable of doing this. It would also fit in with his maintaining an orchard which would benefit the Lloyd family as well as himself, so that the Lloyd family was justified in leaving him the proceeds from his orchard when he was manumitted.

CHAPTER 7

BIOGRAPHICAL SKETCH OF JUPITER HAMMON

By Oscar Wegelin

"MY OLD NEGROES are to be provided for." With these words ends the codicil to the will of Henry Lloyd, owner and lord of Lloyd's Neck, or Queen's Village, dated March 3, 1763.

While these words convey nothing of especial interest in themselves, they are to the student of American literature of paramount importance as among the "old negroes" was a man, a slave, who was destined to become, nay, had already become the first one of his race to see his name in print as a writer of verse in what we are not pleased to call the United States of America.

For without a doubt, Jupiter Hammon, the subject of this volume, was the first member of the Negro race to write and publish poetry in this country. For more than a century Phillis Wheatley has been lauded throughout the English-speaking world as the first of her race to appear in print as a versifier, at least as far as America was concerned. It will be shown however in this sketch of Hammon that not only did he antedate Miss Wheatley by nearly ten years as a poet, but at least one of his poems was printed before she had reached these shores, or knew one work of English.

The earliest trace of Hammon is found in a letter dated 1730, when the poet must have been a child of ten or twelve years. (Ed. Note: he was 19). I give it in full, as follows:

"St. Georges May 19 1730

Sir: I'm informed by Mr Lloyd Jupiter is afflicted wth pains in his Leggs Knees and thighs ascending to his bowels wch in my Esteem is a gouty Rumatick Disorder to releave which and Prevent the Impending Danger (as you observe) of its getting up to his Stomach, Desire the following Directions may be vsed. In the first place give one of the Purges, In the morning fasting, and all night one of the boluses, the next day take away about 12 or 14 ounces of blood (notwithstanding he loost blood in the winter) from the foot will be the most serviceable a day or two after as you find his strength will bear it, give the other purge, and the bolus att night, on those days he doth not purge and is bled give one of the powdrs in the Morning and another in the Evening mixt in some Diet drink made of the equal of Horse Reddish Roots the bark of elder Root Pine Budds or the second bark wood or Toad sorrel, make it stronger with the Ingredients and Lett him drink constantly of it for a month or six weeks and then the remainder of the summer let him have milch whey to drink he must live on a thin spare diet abstaining from meat att nights all spirituous liquors salt pepper and vinegar have sent home oyntmt to be used as he did the former

with my affectionate Regards
to Vncle and Aunt best Respects to all yr good family
I Remain
Your Most Humble and Obedt servt
G. Muirson"

Nearly twenty years ago the late Daniel Parish, Jr., told the writer that he had in his collection a broadside poem written by Hammon which was earlier than anything that had been written by a Negro in America, as far as could be traced. He had, however, mislaid it and could not recall its title. As his statement seemed so remarkable, I at first doubted its correctness, but as this gentleman was well known as an expert among students of early American poetry, I still hoped that what he said would some day be proven. Until his death, which occurred in December of last year, Mr. Parish was unable to find this elusive broadside, and it seemed that it must be forever lost ant the point that I had tried to prove would be forever unsolved. Whenever this "supposed" broadside was mentioned to any of the delvers into the literature of the Colonial period, my surmises regarding Hammon's priority as a poet were received with grave doubt.

I, however, had faith in the statement made by the departed collector and when a few months ago Mr. Chas. Fred. Heartman issued his admirable bibliography of Miss Wheatley, I determined to endeavor once more to locate the long lost broadsheet. With this end in view I wrote to Mr. Robert H. Kelby, Librarian of the New York Historical Society, and inquired of that gentleman if perchance he had discovered among a collection of pamphlets relating to slavery which Mr. Parish had, prior to his death, presented to the society, a broadside poem by one Jupiter Hammon. I described the piece as well as I knew how, expecting that a search would have to be made among a large lot of material. Imagine my surprise when almost immediately I received a reply stating that the broadside that I had been searching for for years was not in the lot of pamphlets presented by Mr. Parish, but was in its proper place among the broadsides belonging to the Society's collection, where it had evidently been for many years.

This was certainly good news, as it proved peradventure that my surmise had been correct, and that Miss Wheatley would have to step down from the pedestal she had so long occupied. My ambition, however, in making this discovery was not to dethrone the dusky versifier of Boston, but I wanted to do justice to one who almost unknown, yet must have been a man of considerable ability and of influence among the members of this own race, bondman though he had been.

Unfortunately, none of his contemporaries seemed to have left behind anything which would throw any light upon his life, in fact the only thing that is known of this interesting character is gathered from his own statements that appear in the most popular of his writings, *An Address to the Negroes of the State of New York*. In this address, which exhorts the slaves to be true to their masters he writes, "When I was in Hartford in Connecticut, where I lived during the War, I published several pieces which were well received, not only by those of my own colour, but by a number of the White people, who thought they might do good among their servants. This is one consideration, among others, that emboldens me now to publish what I have written to you….I am now upwards of seventy years old." This would make the date of his birth about 1720. Where he first saw the light of day, I am unable to state, in fact, were his birth place in Africa, or more probable, the West Indies, he himself was without doubt unable to give the exact date of his natal day. (The letter of Muirson seems to prove that he was born in this country.)

From the tenor of his writings, both poetical and prose, I am inclined to believe with Mr. A. A. Schomburg, that Hammon was a preacher among his people. Mr. Schomburg is almost certain that he preached or led religious gatherings, in Hartford and New Haven. His presence in Hartford during the period of the Revolutionary War is explained by the fact that his master, Joseph Lloyd, was a patriot and was compelled to forsake Long Island when the British and Hessians overran it.

The poem which establishes Hammon's priority as an American Negro versifies, is entitled, "An Evening Thought. Salvation by Christ, with Penetential Cries: Composed by Jupiter Hammon, a Negro belonging to Mr. Lloyd, of Queen's Village, on Long Island, the 25th of December, 1760." It is a broadside, evidently printed at New York early in the following year. The poem comprises 88 lines printed in double column.

Hammon was evidently much interested in Salvation as that word appears no less than twenty-three times in this poem. This slave served no less than three members of the Lloyd family. At the time that his poem was written he was owned by Henry Lloyd, whom he served until the latter's death, which occurred in 1763. (I have mentioned the clause in his will which directed that his Negroes should be cared for.) At his death he left the Neck to his four sons, but Hammon became the property of Joseph, who when the British overran the Island fled to Connecticut. Joseph died during the War and left his part of the Neck to John Lloyd, Jr. This John, who was a grandson of Joseph, became the last owner of Hammon, who at this time was a man of about 60 years of age.

His second publication was a poetical address to Phillis Wheatley, dated "Hartford, August 4, 1778." It is also printed in broadsheet form, and only one copy is known to exist.

His next appearance in print was entitled, "An essay on the Ten Virgins." This was issued at Hartford the following year. I have been unable to locate a copy, but it was advertised as "To be sold" in *The Connecticut Courant*, Dec. 14, 1779.

Nothing new appeared from his pen until 1782, when Hudson & Goodwin printed at Hartford, "A Winter Piece." This was largely in prose, but contained on the last two pages, "A Poem for Children with thoughts on Death."

Hammon was evidently much taken up with thoughts on death, and in his "Address to the Negroes" he writes, "If we should ever get to Heaven, we shall find nobody to reproach us for being black, or for being slaves." Why the if? His next appearance in print was a religious dissertation which he called "An Evening's Improvement." It was printed at Hartford, probably by Hudson & Goodwin, without date, but undoubtedly during the War. It contains a poetical dialogue, entitled, "The Kind Master and Dutiful Servant."

Hammon's masters were evidently kind to him, probably realizing that he was a slave of more than usual intelligence. As will be seen by referring to the list of his writings at the end of this volume, his friends, among whom were undoubtedly some of the members of the Lloyd family, were of assistance to the author in bringing his writings before the public. Without this help, it is doubtful if any of his writings should have seen the light of day, as Hammon was not well enough known to have publishers as anxious to print his writings, as they were, to issue the poems of Phillis Wheatley. While the latter's writings have been issued in many editions, not only in America, but in Europe as well, those of the Long Island slave never reached beyond a single edition, with the exception of the "Address to the Negroes," of which as many as three editions were printed, one after the writer's decease.

Hammon's most important work, probably his last, was not in verse, but was an Address to the Negroes of the state in which he dwelt. Its influence was, however , felt beyond the borders of New York, and we find an edition printed in Philadelphia by Daniel Humphreys the year in which the first made its appearance from the press of Carroll and Patterson. This was in 1787. An edition was also printed in New York, 1806, after the author had ceased to be a slave, and (let us hope) had found rest for his soul in that Heaven he had longed for so often and about which he had written his best lines.

A receipt for money which mentions Hammon is in the New York Historical Society and proves that he was living as late as 1790. I herewith give a copy of it.

"Oysterbay 6th Oct 1790 Recd of John Lloyd Junr twelve Pound in full of the last years Interest on his bond Recd by the hand of Jupiter Hammon & have endorsed it on the Bond

12-0-0   P Loretta Cock"

The year of his death is unknown, but it was between the years 1790 and 1806. In the edition of the Address to the Negroes issued in 1806 three residents of Oyster Bay, Long Island, attest over their own signatures that Hammon was a man of good parts and an esteemed neighbor. The publishers of the 1787 edition state that "They have made no material alterations, in it, except in the spelling, which they found needed considerable correction." By this it will be seen that Hammon was evidently a man without education. How different a career compared with a that of Miss Wheatley, who had the advantages of a good schooling, He, a slave faithfully serving both his Heavenly and earthly Masters, probably almost unknown outside of a small circle in which he moved, while she the child of fortune was petted by all with whom she came in contact. Only an accident prevented her from being introduced to the King of England, George the Third, and the father of his country honored her by sending her an autograph letter.

A few years later, however, she died, broken in spirit, and almost friendless, her later days being darkened through an unfortunate marriage. Her husband, although a man of talent, could not appreciate the gentle and kindly being he had sworn to protect. What would we not give to obtain a likeness of "The Negro Servant of John Lloyd, Jr., of Queen's Village."

Several specimens of the hand-writing of Miss Wheatley are known to exist, but nothing in the chirography of Hammon has been found. (ed. Note: see later poems in Hammon's hand.) Were it not for his printed pamphlets and broadsides his very name would now be forgotten and the first of his race to write verse in America would have none to do him honor. Hammon was, however, the earliest Negro versifier and a not unworthy forerunner of a numerous company of Afro-American poets, the best of whom was the lamented Paul Laurence Dunbar.

In two respects both Hammon and Miss Wheatley were alike. They were both of a deeply religious temperament, and both tried to instill their belief into others. How far they succeeded is not for us to decide, but it seems probable that the exhortations of Hamon to his fellow slaves did meet with success. At any rate his white neighbors seemed pleased with his efforts and did what they could to help him.

Although Hammon must have been well known to some of his

contemporaries, he is almost totally neglected by biographers and bibliographers. Nor is he mentioned in any of the histories of Long Island. The only notices I have found regarding him, beyond the mere mention of his name, are the following:

"Jupiter Hammon, a Negro Slave of Long Island, attained to considerable advancement, both in an intellectual and religious point of view. He published an address to the Negroes of New York, which contains much excellent advice, embodied in language so excellent, that were it not well attested, its genuineness might be justly questioned." Armisted. "A Tribute to the Negro," Manchester, 1848.

"Joseph (Lloyd) had a Negro slave, Jupiter Hammon, who was quite a literary character, and published at Hartford, Dec. '79 an Essay of the Parable of the Ten Virgins." Onderdonk, *Revolutionary Incidents of Queens County.* The present writer contributed to an article on Hammon in the *Literary Collector* for August, 1904. It was headed, "Was Phillis Wheatley America's first black poet?

CHAPTER 8

CRITICAL ANALYSIS OF THE WORKS OF JUPITER HAMMON

By Vernon Loggins

PROBABLY THE FIRST poem published by an American Negro is a broadside of eighty-eight lines entitled *An Evening Thought: Salvation by Christ with Penetential Cries: Composed by Jupiter Hammon, a Negro Belonging to Mr. Lloyd, of Queen's Village, on Long Island, the 25th of December, 1760*. Little is known of Jupiter Hammon. Born about 1720, he lived through the years when the church in America was being democratized, through the period when the Revolution was remaking the thought of the country, and on until the definite establishment of the United States as a nation. All of his life he passed in slavery, belonging, as title-pages of his publications attest, to three different members of the Lloyd family of Long Island. Except for the time during the War of the Revolution when the British were in possession of Long Island and the patriot Lloyds with their slaves were in exile in Hartford, Connecticut, Jupiter Hammon's residence was probably on the Lloyd estate near Queen's Village. Aside from his own statement that he was "able to do almost any kind of business," there seem to be no records giving information regarding his exact status as a slave; and we do not know whether he was a farm laborer, a household servant, or a workman at some trade.

The Lloyds were evidently humane and considerate masters; for Hammon, addressing his fellow slaves, wrote in 1786:

"I have good reason to be thankful that my lot is so much better than most slaves have had.

I suppose I have had more advantages than most of you who are slaves have ever known, and I believe more than many white people have enjoyed."

Whatever advantages and privileges the Lloyds might have granted him, there is no indication in his writings that they gave him opportunity for instruction beyond the most elementary training in reading and writing. But they undoubtedly allowed him to go freely to church, where he absorbed the doctrines of the Calvinistic Methodists, of which all of his work is an echo. His masters also, it seems, left him free at times to engage in preaching. Stimulated by religious indulgences, he read with avidity the Bible and hymn books and possibly such pious poems as Michael Wigglesworth's *The Day of Doom*. It was in all probability through this reading that he taught himself what he knew about prose style and the art of versification.

Hammon said in 1786: "When I was at Hartford, in Connecticut, where I lived during the war, I published several pieces which were well received, not only by those of my own color, but by a number of the white people, who thought they might do good among the servants." *An Address to Miss Phillis Wheatly,* a poem of twenty-one ballad stanzas, appeared as a broadside in 1778. In 1779, came *An Essay on the Ten Virgins,* of which no copy seems to exist. That it was published, however, is scarcely to be doubted, since it was advertised in the *Connecticut Courant* for December 14, 1779. *A Winter Piece,* a sermon in prose with "A Poem for Children with Thoughts on Death" tacked on at the end, appeared in pamphlet form in 1782. Another prose pamphlet, *An Evening's Improvement,* including also a dialogue in verse entitled "The Kind Master and the Dutiful Servant," was published at Hartford without date. These four pieces written during the Revolution, with *An Evening Thought* (1760) and *An Address to the Negroes of the State of New-York* (1787), make up all of the known writings of Jupiter Hammon. That he produced other broadsides and pamphlets of which there is at present no apparent trace is altogether possible.

It is an interesting coincidence that most of Hammon's poetry was published at Hartford at a time when that Connecticut town was the literary capital of America. But if the neoclassical "Hartford Wits" read his poems, they no doubt looked upon them as chaotic effusions of crude thoughts poured out in a verse not inappropriate to the cheapest balladry. To the twentieth-century mind, which places a high value on the artlessness of folk poetry, Jupiter Hammon's work takes on a new meaning. There is a strength of wild and native religious feeling in what he wrote, a strength which he achieved without conscious effort. From hearing evangelical sermons and from reading the Bible according to his own untrained fancy, he picked up strange notions regarding salvation, penitential cries, redeeming love, tribunal day, the Holy Word, bounteous mercies. His mystic Negro mind played with these notions; and, endowed with the instinct for music which is so strong in his race, he sang out his impressions in such meters as he had become familiar with in the hymns of Charles Wesley and Augustus Montague Toplady, and in such rimes as for the moment pleased his ear. Indeed, his method of composition must have been that of the unknown maker of the spirituals.

Like the spirituals, the poems of Jupiter Hammon were composed to be heard. There is evident in his verse that peculiar sense for sound which is the most distinguishing characteristic of Negro folk poetry. A word that appeals to his ear he uses over and over again, in order, it seems, to cast a spell with it. In *An Evening Thought* the word *salvation* occurs in every three or four lines. Any impressionable sinners who might have heard Jupiter Hammon chant the poem when in the ecstasy of religious emotion no doubt went away to be haunted by the sound of the word *salvation* if not by the idea. A few lines will illustrate the effectiveness of the repetition:

Salvation comes now from the Lord,
Our victorious King,
His holy name be well ador'd,
Salvation surely bring.
Dear Jesus give thy spirit now,
Thy grace to every Nation,
That han't the Lord to whom we bow,
The author of Salvation.
Dear Jesus, unto Thee we cry,
Give us the preparation;
Turn not away thy tender eye;
We seek thy true Salvation.

In the original broadside the poem was printed, as here quoted, without a break between stanzas; However, the metrical arrangement is that of the ballad stanza with alternating rimes, a verse form which is often found in the early Methodist hymns, and which is the basis for the stanza in Wigglesworth's *the Day of Doom*. Hammon followed this pattern in all of his poems, though not without marked irregularities. There are numerous cases of wrenched accents demanding an outrageous pronunciation. There are many examples of syncopation, so characteristic of Negro dance rhythms, evident in the omission at times of one syllable and at other times of two, as in the following line, which is supposed to be tetrameter:

Thou mightst been left behind.

But the most interesting irregularities are the strange rime combinations – such as *word* and *God, Lord* and *God, call* and *soul, sound* and *down*. Since we know little about how English was spoken by the Negroes on Long Island in the eighteenth century, we cannot determine how far astray Jupiter Hammon's was in hearing exact rimes in such combinations. We can say with definiteness that the riming words which he selected are always sonorous.

While the imagery in Hammon's poems is in general restrained, often taken bodily from the New Testament, there are unexpected turns in the thought which suggest the wild extravagance of the spiritual. The unusual association of ideas in the following stanza from *An Address to Miss Phillis Wheatly* is probably the result of a necessity for rimes;

> God's tender mercy brought thee here;
> Tost o'er the raging main;
> In Christian faith thou hast a share,
> Worth all the gold of Spain.

The last three lines of the following stanza from the same poem might not seem out of place in a spiritual;

> That thou a pattern still might be,
>   To youth of Boston town,
> The blessed Jesus set thee free
>   From every sinful wound.

In two stanzas of "A Poem for Children with Thoughts on Death" Hammon pictures the dread terror of the day of final judgment. Back of the ominous words of warning to sinful children there is a delightful feeling of playfulness, suggestive of a traditional Southern many threatening a willful infant with the imminent approach of a voodoo man.

> Then shall ye hear the trumpet sound,
> The graves give up their dead,

Those blessed saints shall quick awake,
  And leave their dusty beds.
Then shall ye hear the trumpet sound,
  And rend the native sky,
Those bodies starting from the ground,
  In the twinkling of an eye.

In "The Kind Master and the Dutiful Servant," written in dialogue, a form which indicates that the author might have known something of the English popular ballad, Hammon suddenly leaves the drama six stanzas from the end and naively addresses his readers in his own person.

Believe me now, my Christian friends,
  Believe your friend call'd Hammon:
You cannot to your God attend,
  And serve the God of Mammon.

It must not be supposed that Jupiter Hammon was only primitive and naïve, merely a folk poet incapable of consistent and orderly reflection. *An Address to Miss Phillis Wheatly,* his second poem, written eighteen years after his first spontaneous and chaotic effort, *An Evening Thought,* shows a balanced structure of ideas, based on the theme that it was a divine providence which brought Phillis Wheatly from heathen Africa to a land where she could know the true religion and teach it to others. Both this poem and "A Poem for Children with Thoughts on Death" are provided with scriptural glosses, and in each the thought associated with the Biblical citations is fairly logical and exact. While the two earlier prose pamphlets, *A Winter Piece* and An Evening's Improvement, intended as sermons, are rhapsodic and incoherent, the *Address to the Negroes in the State of New-York* displays a regular and firm organization. It opens with personal reminiscences, and these are followed by a series of moral precepts. Negroes are admonished to be obedient and faithful to their masters, to be honest and not to steal, to be energetic and not to dally when sent on errands, to be always religious and never profane. In the closing section, which deals with the subject of freedom for the slaves, Hammon praises the blessings of liberty. But concerning his own condition of slavery he mildly concludes:

"Now I acknowledge that liberty is a great thing, and worth seeking for, if we can get it honestly; and by our good conduct prevail on our masters to set us free: though for my own part I do not wish to be free; for many of us who are grown up slaves, and have always had masters to take care of us, should hardly know how to take care of themselves; and it may be for our own comfort to remain as we are."

Perhaps because of this conciliatory attitude toward slavery, Jupiter Hammon's work was disregarded by the early Negro leaders, who in most cases kept alive the personalities of the predecessors of any distinction whatsoever. The name of America's first Negro poet dropped into oblivion soon after his death, to remain there for more than a century. His attempts at thoughtful composition, such as *An Address to the Negroes in the State of New-York,* fall low in the class of the subliterary. It is his poetry, with all of its artlessness and crudeness, which makes his name important. As the product of the uncultivated Negro imagination and temperament, his verse, slight as the body of it is, forms a unique contribution to American poetry in the eighteenth century. The reader of today is likely to find a more sincere feeling in it than in most religious verse written in America during Hammon's age. It is a quaint prelude to the rich and varied songs which were to burst spontaneously from the Negro folk a little later, songs which make up the great gift from Africa to the art of America.

A N

Evening THOUGHT.

SALVATION BY *CHRIST*,

WITH

PENETENTIAL CRIES:

Composed by Jupiter Hammon, a Negro belonging to Mr Lloyd, of Queen's-
Village, on Long-Island, the 25th of December, 1760.

SALVATION comes by Jesus Christ alone,
　The only Son of God ;
Redemption now to every one,
　That love his holy Word.
Dear Jesus we would fly to Thee,
　And leave off every Sin,
Thy tender Mercy well agree ;
　Salvation from our King.
Salvation comes now from the Lord,
　Our victorious King ;
His holy Name be well ador'd,
　Salvation surely bring.
Dear Jesus give thy Spirit now,
　Thy Grace to every Nation,
That thin't the Lord to whom we bow,
　The Author of Salvation.
Dear Jesus unto Thee we cry,
　Give us thy Preparation,
Turn not away thy tender Eye;
　We seek thy true Salvation.
Salvation comes from God we know,
　The true and only One;
It's well agreed and certain true,
　He gave his only Son.
Lord hear our penetential Cry :
　Salvation from above ;
It is the Lord that doth supply,
　With his Redeeming Love.
Dear Jesus by thy precious Blood,
　The World Redemption have:
Salvation comes now from the Lord,
　He being thy captive Slave.
Dear Jesus let the Nations cry,
　And all the People say,
Salvation comes from Christ on high,
　Haste on Tribunal Day.
We cry as Sinners to the Lord,
　Salvation to obtain ;
It is firmly fixt his holy Word,
　Ye shall not cry in vain.
Dear Jesus unto Thee we cry,
　And make our Lamentation :
O let our Prayers ascend on high ;
　We felt thy Salvation.

Lord turn our dark benighted Souls ;
　Give us a true Motion,
And let the Hearts of all the World,
　Make Christ their Salvation.
Ten Thousand Angels cry to Thee,
　Yea louder than the Ocean.
Thou art the Lord, we plainly see ;
　Thou art the true Salvation.
Now is the Day, excepted Time ;
　The Day of Salvation ;
Increase your Faith, do not repine :
　Awake ye every Nation.
Lord unto whom now shall we go,
　Or seek a safe Abode ;
Thou hast the Word Salvation too
　The only Son of God.
Ho ! every one that hunger hath,
　Or pineth after me,
Salvation be thy leading Staff,
　To set the Sinner free.
Dear Jesus unto Thee we fly ;
　Depart, depart from Sin,
Salvation doth at length supply,
　The Glory of our King.
Come ye Blessed of the Lord,
　Salvation gently given ;
O turn your Hearts, accept the Word,
　Your Souls are fit for Heaven.
Dear Jesus we now turn to Thee,
　Salvation to obtain ;
Our Hearts and Souls do meet again,
　To magnify thy Name.
Come holy Spirit, Heavenly Dove,
　The Object of our Care ;
Salvation doth increase our Love ;
　Our Hearts hath felt thy fear.
Now Glory be to God on High,
　Salvation high and low ;
And thus the Soul on Christ rely,
　To Heaven surely go.
Come Blessed Jesus, Heavenly Dove,
　Accept Repentance here ;
Salvation give, with tender Love ;
　Let us with Angels share.

F I N I S.

CHAPTER 9

AN EVENING THOUGHT: SALVATION BY CHRIST, WITH PENETENTIAL CRIES:

COMPOSED BY JUPITER Hammon, a Negro belonging to Mr. Lloyd, of Queen's-Village, on Long-Island, the 25th of December, 1760.

Salvation comes by Jesus Christ alone,
   The only Son of God;
Redemption now to every one,
   That love his holy Word.
Dear Jesus we would fly to Thee,
   And leave off every Sin,
Thy tender Mercy well agree;
   Salvation from our King.
Salvation comes now from the Lord,
   Our victorious King:
His holy Name be well ador'd,
   Salvation surely bring.
Dear Jesus give thy Spirit now,
   Thy Grace to every Nation,

That han't the Lord to whom we bow,
  The Author of Salvation.
Dear Jesus unto Thee we cry,
  Give us the Preparation:
Turn not away thy tender Eye;
  We seek thy true Salvation.
Salvation comes from God we know,
  The true and only One;
It's well agreed and certain true,
  He gave his only Son.
Lord hear our penetential Cry:
  Salvation from above;
It is the Lord that doth supply,
  With his Redeeming Love.
Dear Jesus by thy precious Blood,
  The World Redemption have:
Salvation now comes from the Lord,
  He being thy captive slave.
Dear Jesus let the Nations cry,
  And all the people say,
Salvation comes from Christ on high,
  Haste on Tribunal Day.
We cry as Sinners to the Lord,
  Salvation to obtain;
It is firmly fixt his holy Word,
  Ye shall not cry in vain.
Dear Jesus unto Thee we cry,
  And make our Lamentation:
O let our Prayers ascend on high;
  We felt thy Salvation.
Lord turn our dark benighted Souls;
  Give us a true Motion,

And let the Hearts of all the World,
  Make Christ their Salvation.
Ten Thousand Angels cry to Thee,
  Yea louder than the Ocean.
Thou art the Lord, we plainly see;
  Thou art the true Salvation.
Now is the Day, excepted Time;
  The Day of Salvation;
Increase your Faith, do not repine:
  Awake ye every Nation.
Lord unto whom now shall we go,
  Or seek a safe Abode;
Thou hast the Word Salvation too
  The only Son of God.
Ho! every one that hunger hath,
  Or pineth after me,
Salvation be thy leading Staff,
  To set the Sinner free.
Dear Jesus unto Thee we fly;
  Depart, depart from Sin,
Salvation doth at length supply,
  The Glory of our King.
Come ye Blessed of the Lord,
  Salvation greatly given;
O turn your Hearts, accept the Work,
  Your Souls are fit for Heaven.
Dear Jesus we now turn to Thee,
  Salvation to obtain;
Our Hearts and Souls do meet again,
  To magnify thy Name.
Come holy Spirit, Heavenly Dove,
  The Object of our Care;
Salvation doth increase our Love;
  Our Hearts hath felt thy fear.

Now Glory be to God on High,
　　Salvation high and low;
And thus the Soul on Christ rely,
　　To Heaven surely go.
Come Blessed Jesus, Heavenly Dove,
　　Accept repentance here;
Salvation give, with tender Love;
　　Let us with Angels share.

Come ye youth of Boston town
the mournfull News youll hear
the Pious youth though just come on   } Sickness {
Shall Quickly Disappear

She Always did appear to be
A Chosen Child of god
he Gave her Grace that Set her free
She Loved his holy Word

In Wisdoms ways She always went
an Gave a Just Record
for Every Sin She Should Repent
and fly unto the Lord

She Like a Lamb & mournfull Dove
She Silently did Cry
Dear Jesus Come ye from above
My Soul on thee Rely

She did Confirm the Holy word
to youth that Live in Sin
to Leave that way and Serve the Lord
that Christ may take them in

She going the way of all the Earth
her Nature doth Decay
Dear Jesus Send her thy Relief
And help her now to Pray

Not many days before the word
her Panting heart did fly
She thus Prayed unto the Lord
And met a fresh Reply

Come Blessed Jesus now Look down
have mercy on my Soul
and thus forgive the Sins ive Done
and Quickly Send thy Call

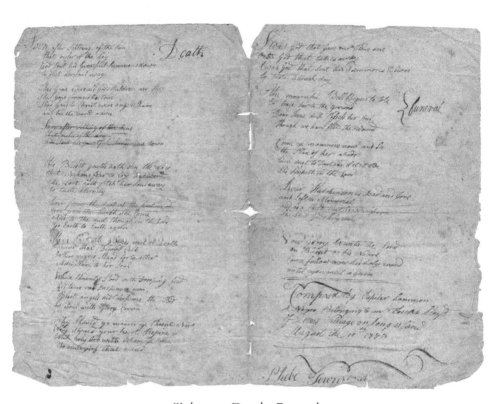

Sickness, Death, Funeral
Hillhouse Family Papers (MS 282),
Manuscript and Archives, Yale University Library.

CHAPTER 10

SICKNESS, DEATH, AND FUNERAL

A Poem Composed by Jupiter Hammon

SICKNESS

Come Ye youth of Boston Town
The Mournfull News youl hear
The Pious youth though just
come on
Shall Quickly Disappear

She Always did appear to be
A Chosen Child of god
He gave her grace that set her
free
She Loved his holy Word

In Wisdoms ways She always
went
an gave a just Record
for every Sin She should Repent
And fly unto the Lord

She Like a Lamb or mournful
dove
She Silently did cry
Dear Jesus Come ye from above
My Soul on the Rely

She did Confirm the Holy work
To youth that live in sin
To Leave that way and Serve the
Lord
That Christ may take them in

She going the way of all the
Earth
Her nature doth Decay
Dear Jesus send her thy Relief
And help her now to Pray

Not many days before the word
Her Panting heart did fly
She thus Prayed unto the Lord
And met a fresh Reply

Come Blessed Jesus now look
down
Have mercy on my Soul
And thus forgive the ills i've done
And Quickly send thy Call

DEATH

Soon after setting of the sun
That ruler of the day
God sent his greatful summons
down
to fleet her soul away

She's past the gloomy vail of
Death
Received that Blessed pall
Where angels stand for to attend
admittance to her soul

She's gone where all God's chil-
dren are
She's gone from us 'tis true
She's gone to Christ wear angels
share
and bid the world adieu

while Parent stood with
Drooping head
his tears now Dropping down
blest angels did perfume the bed
the soul with Glory crown

this Blessed youth hath join the
day
that Nations fear to try
the Lord hath fetch her soul
away
to taste Eternity

Why should ye mourn ye Parent
Now
Why should your heart Repine
With holy Job with whom ye
Rows
be now of that mind

'Twas from the dust at the first
word
Yea, from the Earth she came
And to the dust though in the
Lord
Go Earth to Earth again

'Twas God that gave our Pious
one
for 'tis God that takes away
'twas God that sent his summons
Down
to taste Eternal day

FUNERAL

The mournful Bell begins to tole
To trace her to the ground
Dear Jesus doth possess her soul
Though we have felt the wound

Come ye mourners now and See
the place of her abode
turn dust to dust and let it be
She Sleepeth in the Lord

Dear Hutchinson is dead and Gone
and left a Memorial
And as a Child that is newborn
The Lord God's holy wil

Now Glory be unto the Lord
and Blessed be his Name
Come follow now his holy work
Until you meet again

Composed by Jupiter hammon
a Negro Belonging to Mr. Joseph Lloyd of
Queens Village on Long Island
august the 10th 1770

Phebe Townsend

CHAPTER 11

AN ADDRESS TO MISS PHILLIS WHEATLEY

I

O come you pious youth! Adore
The wisdom of thy God,
In bringing thee from distant shore
To learn His holy word.

Eccles. xii.

II

Thou mightst been left behind
Amidst a dark abode;
God's tender mercy still combin'd,
Thou hast the holy word.

Psal. cxxxv. 2, 3.

III

Fair wisdom's ways are paths of peace,
And they that walk therein,
Shall reap the joys that never cease,
And Christ shall be their king.

Psal. i. 1, 2; Prov. iii, 7

IV

God's tender mercy brought thee here;
Tost o'er the raging main;
In Christian faith thou hast a share,
Worth all the gold of Spain.

Psal. ciii, 1, 3, 4.

V

While thousands tossed by the sea,
And others settled down,
God's tender mercy set thee free,
From dangers that come down.

Death.

VI

That thou a pattern still might be,
To youth of Boston town,
The blessed Jesus set thee free,
From every sinful wound.

2 Cor. v. 10.

VII

The blessed Jesus, who came down,
Unvail'd his sacred face,
To cleanse the soul of every wound,
And give repenting grace.

Rom. v. 21.

VIII

That we poor sinners may obtain,
The pardon of our sin;
Dear blessed Jesus now constrain,
And bring us flocking in.

Psal. xxxiv. 6, 7, 8.

IX

Come you, Phillis, now aspire,
And seek the living God,
So step by step thou mayst go higher,
Till perfect in the word.

Matth. vii, 7, 8.

X

While thousands mov'd to distant shore,
And others left behind,
The blessed Jesus still adore,
Implant this in thy mind.

Psal. lxxix. 1.

XI

Thou hast left the heathen shore;
Thro' mercy of the Lord,
Among the heathen live no more,
Come magnify thy God.

Psal. xxxiv. 1, 2, 3.

XII

I pray the living God may be
The shepherd of thy soul;
His tender mercies still are free,
His mysteries to unfold.

Psal. lxxx. 1, 2, 3.

XIII

Thou, Phillis, when thou hunger hast,
Or pantest for thy God;
Jesus Christ is thy relief,
Thou hast the holy word.

Psal. xiii. 1, 2, 3.

XIV

The bounteous mercies of the Lord,
Are hid beyond the sky,
And holy souls that love His word,
Shall taste them when they die.

Psal. xvi, 10, 11.

XV

These bounteous mercies are from God,
The merits of His Son;
The humble soul that loves His word,
He chooses for His own.

Psal. xxxiv. 15.

XVI

Come, dear Phillis, be advis'd,
To drink Samaria's flood;
There nothing that shall suffice
But Christ's redeeming blood.

John iv. 13, 14.

XVII

While thousands muse with earthly toys;
And range about the street,
Dear Phillis, seek for heaven's joys,
Where we do hope to meet.

Matth. vi. 33.

XVIII

When God shall send his summons down,
And number saints together,
Blest angels chant, (triumphant sound),
Come live with me forever.

Psal. cxvi. 15.

XIX

The humble soul shall fly to God,
And leave the things of time,
Start forth as 'twere at the first word,
To taste things more divine.

Matth. v. 3, 8.

XX

Behold! the soul shall waft away,
Whene'er we come to die,
And leave its cottage made of clay,
In twinkling of an eye.

Cor. xv. 51, 52, 53.

XXI

Now glory be to the Most High,
United praises given,
By all on earth, incessantly,
And all the host of heav'n.

Psal. cl. 6.

CHAPTER 12

AN EVENING'S IMPROVEMENT

John I. 29.
--Behold the Lamb of God which taketh
away the sins of the world.

IN THE BEGINNING of this chapter John bears testimony, that Jesus is the Son of God. Verse 1ˢᵗ· In the beginning was the word, and the word was with God, and the word was God. This is that Lamb of God which I now invite you to behold. My Brethren, we are to behold the Son of God as our Lord and giver of life; for he was made flesh and dwelt among us, verse 14 of the context, and here he is declared to be the Son of God full of grace and truth. And here in the first place I mean to shew the necessity of beholding the Lamb of God in the sense of the text. 2ⁿᵈ Endeavour to shew when we are said to behold the Son of God in the sense of the text. 3ʳᵈ. I shall shew when we may be said not to behold the Lamb of God as we should do. In the 4ᵗʰ place I shall endeavor to shew how far we may be mistaken in beholding the Lamb of God. In the 5ᵗʰ place I shall endeavor to rectify these mistakes.

My brethren, since I wrote my Winter Piece it hath been requested that I would write something more for the advantage of my friends, by my superiors, gentlemen, whose judgment I depend on, and by my friends in general, I have had an invitation to give a public exhortation; but did not think it my duty at that time; but now, my brethren, by divine assistance, I shall endeavor to shew the necessity of beholding the Lamb of God. My brethren we must behold the Lamb of God as taking away the sin of the world, as in our text, and it is necessary that we behold the Lamb of God as our King: ah! as the King immortal, eternal, invisible, as the only Son of God, for he hath declared him, as in the 8th verse of the context, no man hath seen God at any time: the only begotten Son, which is in the bosom of the Father, he hath declared him. My brethren, let us strive to behold the Lamb of God, with faith and repentance; to come weary and heavy laden with our sin, for they have made us unworthy of the mercy of the Lamb of God; therefore, we see now necessary it is that we behold the Lamb of God, in the sense of the text, that is, in a spiritual manner, not having on our own righteousness; but we must be cloathed upon, with the unspotted robes of the Lamb of God; we must work out our salvation with fear and trembling, always abounding in the works of the Lord; we must remember the vows of our baptism, which is to follow the Lamb of God. John Chap. 1. 33, speaking of baptism, he saith, upon whom thou shalt see the spirit descending and remaining on him, the same is he which baptiseth with the Holy Ghost, and verse 34, and I saw, and bare record, that this is the Son of God, verse 35, again the next day after, John stood and two of his disciples heard him speak and they followed Jesus. Thus, my dear brethren, we are to follow the Lamb of God, at all times, whether in prosperity or adversity, knowing that all things work together for good, to them that love God, or as in Rom. viii. 28. Now let us manifest that we love God, by a holy life; let us strive to glorify and magnify the name of the most high God. It is necessary that we behold the Lamb of God, by taking heed to our ways, that we sin not with our tongues, Psalm xxxix. 1. Here, my brethren, we have the exhortation of David, who beheld the Lamb of God with faith and love, for he crys out with a most humble petition, O Lord, rebuke me not in thine anger; neither chastise me in thy hot displeasure. Psalm vi. 1. And now, by brethren, have we not great reason to cry to the Lamb of God, that taketh away the sin of the world, that he may have mercy on us and forgive us our sins, and that he would give us his holy spirit, that we may have such hungerings and thirsting as may be acceptable in the sight of God; for as the heart panteth for the water brook, so should our souls pant for the living God. Psalm xlii. 1. and now, my brethren, we must behold the law of God, as is exprest, John I. 51. And he saith unto him, verily, verily I say unto you, hereafter you shall see heaven open, and the angels of God ascending and descending upon the Son of Man. This is a representation of the great day, when the Lamb of God shall appear. Matt. xxiv. 30, and then shall appear the sign of the Son of Man in heaven and then shall the tribes of the earth mourn, and they shall see the Son of Man coming in the clouds of heaven, with power and great glory. Here my brethren, we have life and death set before us, for if we mourn with the tribes for our sins, which have made us unworthy of the least favour in the sight of God, then he will have mercy and he will give us his holy spirit; then we shall have hearts to pray to the Lamb of God, as David did when he was made sensible of his imperfections, then he cryed to the Lamb of God, have mercy upon me O God. Psal. lxi. 1, according to thy loving kindness, according to the multitude of thy tender mercies, blot out my transgressions. This my brethren is the language of the penitent, for he hath a desire that his heart may be turned from darkness to light, from sin to holiness; this none can do but God; for the carnal mind is enmity against God, for it is not subject to the law of God, neither can be. Here we see that we must behold the Lamb of God as calling to us in the most tender and compassionate manner, Matt. xxiii. 37, saying, O Jerusalem, Jerusalem, how often would I have gathered thy children together, even as a hen gathereth her chickens under her wings, and ye would not. As much as if he had said, O ye wicked and rebellious people have I not sent the ministers of the gospel to teach you, and you will not receive the doctrine of the gospel, which is faith and repentance, I tell you nay; but except ye repent ye shall all likewise perish, Luke

xiii. 4.

And now my dear brethren, have we repented of our sins? Have we not neglected to attend divine service? Or if we have attended to the word of God, have we been sincere? For God is a spirit, and they that worship him must worship him in spirit and truth, John iv. 24. When we have heard the word of God sounding in our ears, inviting of us to behold the Lamb of God; O my dear brethren, have we as it were laid up these words in our hearts, or have we not been like the stony ground hearers? Matt. xii. 20. But he that received the seed into stony places, the same is he that heareth the word, and anon with joy receiveth it. Ver. 21. Yet hath not root in himself, but dureth for a while; for when tribulation or persecution ariseth because of the word, by and by he is offended. This is the effect of a hard heart. There is such a depravity in our natures that we are not willing to suffer any reproach that may be cast on us for the sake of our religion; this my brethren is because we have not the love of God shed abroad in our hearts; but our hearts are set too much on the pleasures of this life, forgetting that they are passing away; but the children of God are led by the spirit of God. Rom. viii. 12, Therefore brethren we are debtors, not to the flesh to live after the flesh. Ver. 13. For if ye live after the flesh ye shall die; but if through the spirit do mortify the deeds of the body, ye shall live. Ver. 14, For as many are led by the spirit of God, they are the sons of God. Here my brethren we see that it is our indispensable duty to conform to the will of God in all things, not having our hearts set on the pleasures of this life; but we must prepare for death, our great and last change. For we are sinners by nature, and are adding thereunto by evil practices, for man is prone to evil as the sparks fly upward; and there is nothing short of the divine power of the most high God can turn our hearts to see the living and true God; and now we ought to behold the Lamb of God, as it is expressed in Isaiah vii.14, A virgin shall conceive and bear a son, and shall call his name Emanuel. This my brethren is the Son of God, who died to save us guilty sinners, and it is only by the mercy of the blessed Jesus we can be saved: Therefore, let us cast off self-dependence, and rely on a crucified Saviour, whose blood was shed for all that came unto him by faith and repentance; this we cannot do of ourselves, but we must be found in the use of means; therefore we ought to come as David did, Psal. li. 1, Have mercy on me O God, according to thy loving kindness. This my brethren is the duty of all flesh to come to the divine fountain, and to confess our sins before the most high God; for if we say we have no sin we deceive ourselves and the truth is not in us; but if we confess our sins he is faithful and just to forgive us our transgressions. And now my brethren, seeing I have had an invitation to write something more to encourage my dear fellow servants and brethren, Africans, in the knowledge of the Christian religion, I must beg your patience, for I mean to use the utmost brevity that so important a subject will admit of; and now my brethren, we have, as I observed in the foregoing part of this discourse, life and death set before us, for we are invited to come and accept of Christ on the terms of the gospel. Isaiah xliv. 1, O every one that thirsteth, come ye to the waters, and he that hath no money, come ye buy and eat, yea, come ye buy wine and milk, without money and without price. Here is life, and if we search our hearts, and try our ways, and turn again unto the Lord he will forgive us our sins and blot out our transgressions, Lamen. lii. 40. But if we continue in our sins, having our hearts set on the pleasures of this life, forgetting that we must give an account for the deeds done in the body. Psal. lxii. 12, Also unto the Lord belongeth mercy, for he rendereth to every man according to his works. Here we see that we should behold the Lamb of God by a holy life. Psal. vii. 11, God judgeth the righteous and is angry with the wicked every day, ver. 12, if he turn not. He will whet his sword, he hath bent his bow and made it ready. Here we see that the wrath of God abideth on the unbelievers and unconverted sinner. And now my brethren, should not a sense of these things make us cry out in the apostle's language, 'Men and brethren what shall we do to be saved?' We must be found in the use of means, and pray that God would be pleased to rain down a rain of righteousness into our souls; then we shall behold the Lamb of God as taking away the sins of the world. Let us my brethren examine ourselves whether we have had a saving change wrought in our hearts, and have been brought to bow to the divine sovereignty of a crucified Saviour; have we been brought to behold the Lamb of God, by obeying the precepts of Isaiah, and turning from evil and learning to do well. Isaiah i. 16, Wash ye, make you clean; put away the evil of your doing from before mine eyes; cease to do evil, learn to do well. Here we have the admonition of the prophet Isaiah, who was inspired with the knowledge of divine things, so that he calls heaven and earth to witness against the wicked and rebellious sinner. Isaiah i. 2, Here O heavens and give ear O earth; for the Lord hath spoken, I have nourished up children, and they have rebelled against me. Is not this the case? Have we not been going astray like lost sheep? Luke xv. 6, Have we not great reason to lay our hands on our mouths and our mouths in the dust, and come upon the bended knees of our souls and beg for mercy as the publican did, saying, God be merciful to me a sinner, Luke viii.13. This my dear brethren should be the language of our conversation; to have a life void of offence towards God and towards man. Have we beheld the Lamb of God, by taking up our cross, denying ourselves, and following the blessed Jesus. Matt. xvi. 24, Then said Jesus unto his disciples, if any man will be my disciple, let him deny himself, take up his cross and follow me. Here we see that we should behold the Lamb of God as our only Saviour and mighty Redeemer, and we are to take up our cross and follow the Lamb of God at all times, not to murmur at the hand of Divine Providence; and we have our example set before us, Luke xxii. 41, 42, And he was withdrawn from them about a stone's cast, and he kneeled down and prayed, saying, my Father, if thou be willing, remove this cup from me, nevertheless not my will but thine be done. We should behold the Lamb of God as coming in the clouds of heaven with great power and glory, whom our heavenly Father hath declared to be his only Son. Matt. xvii. 5, And while he yet spoke, behold a bright cloud overshadowed them; and behold a voice out of the cloud which said, this is my beloved Son in whom I am well pleased, hear him. Should not a sense of these things inflame our hearts with fear and love to God; knowing that there is no other name given by which we can be saved, but by the name of Jesus; let us behold the Lamb of God as having power to make the blind to see, the dumb to speak, and the lame to walk, and even to raise the dead: But it may be objected and said by those that have had the advantage of studying, are we to expect miracles at this day? These things were done to confirm that Jesus was the Son of God, and to free us from the burthen of types and ceremonies of the Jewish law; and this by way of instruction, which I desire to receive with an humble spirit. Others may object and say, what can we expect from an unlearned Ethiopian? And this by way of reflection. To this I answer, Pray Sir, give me leave to ask this question, Doth not the raising of Lazarus give us a sight of our sinful natures? John xi. 12, 13, And when he had thus spoken, he said with a loud voice, Lazarus come forth. Ver. 4, And he that was dead came forth, bound hand and foot with grave clothes, and his head was bound with a napkin; Jesus saith unto them, loose him and let him go. Is not this a simile of our deadness by nature? And there is nothing short of the power of the most high God can rise us to life. Sirs, I know we are not to expect miracles at this day; but hear the words of our Saviour. Matt. xvi, And Simon Peter answered and said, thou art Christ the Son of the living God. Ver. 17, And Jesus answered and said unto him, blessed art thou Simon Barjona, for flesh and blood hath not revealed it unto thee, but my Father which is in heaven. Sirs, this may suffice to prove that it is by grace we are saved, and that not of ourselves, is the gift of God. But my brethren, for whom this discourse is designed, I am now in the second place to shew when we are said to behold the Lamb of God in the sense of the text: When we are brought humbly to confess our sins, before the most high God, and are calling on our souls and all that is within us to bless his holy name; this is the duty of all flesh, to praise God for his unmerited mercy in giving his Son to save lost man, who by the fall of Adam became guilty in the sight of God. Rom. v. 8, But God commandeth his love towards us in that while we were sinners Christ died for us. Here we are to behold the Lamb of God as suffering for our sins, and it is only by the precious blood of Christ we can be saved, when we are made sensible of our own imperfections and are desirous to love and fear God; this we cannot do of ourselves, for this is the work of God's holy spirit. John vi. 64, And he said, therefore said I unto you that no man can come unto me except it were given unto him of my Father. Here we see to behold the Lamb of God, in the sense of the text, as the gift of God; we should come as David did, saying, O Lord rebuke me not in thine anger, neither chastise me in thy hot displeasure, Psal. vi. 1. And we should put our whole trust in the Lord at all times; we should strive to live a religious life, to avoid the very appearance of evil, least we incur the wrath of God. Psal. xi. 6, Upon the wicked he shall rain showers of fire and brimstone, and an horrible tempest; this shall be the portion of their cup. Here we see the unhappy state of the sinner; for he is not only led away by that subtle adversary the devil, but he hath the word of God pronounced against him. Matt. xxv. 40, Then shall he say unto them on the left hand depart from me ye cursed into everlasting fire prepared for the devil and his angels. Here my brethren we are to behold the Lamb of God as being crucified for us. Matt. xxiii. 20, Pilate therefore willing to release Jesus spake again to them. Ver. 22, But they cryed, saying crucify him, crucify him. Here we see the effect of sin; the blood of Christ was shed for all that came unto him by faith and repentance. O my brethren, when those things have a proper influence on our minds, by the power of the most high God, to say as David did, Psal. ciii. 1, Bless the Lord O my soul, and forget not all his benefits. Then we may be said to behold the Lamb of God in the sense of the text: And we are to behold the Lamb of God as it is expressed in Matt. xvii. 22, And while they abode in Galilee Jesus said unto them, the Son of Man shall be betrayed into the hands of men; and ver. 23, And they shall kill him, and the third day he shall rise again. And now should not a sense of these things have a tendency to make us humble in the sight of God, and we should see the place and situation of Christ suffering. Luke xxii. 33, And when they were come to the place called Calvary, there they crucified him, and the malefactors one on the right hand

and the other on the left. Here we see the boundless riches of free grace; he is numbered with transgressors, whose blood speaks better things than the blood of Abel; for the blood of Abel calls for justice on the sinner, but the blood of Christ calls for mercy. Luke xxiii. 34, Then said Jesus, Father forgive them, for they know not what they do. Here we have the example of our Saviour, that we should forgive our enemies, and pray that God would forgive them also, or how shall we say the Lord's Prayer, 'Forgive us our trespasses as we forgive them that trespass against us.' Now when we are enabled to do these things, as we should do them, then may we be said to behold the Lamb of God in the sense of the text. And now by dear brethren, I am to remind you of a most melancholy scene of Providence; it hath pleased the most high God, in his wise providence, to permit a cruel and unnatural war to be commenced; let us examine ourselves whether we have not been the cause of this heavy judgment; have we been truly thankful for mercies bestowed? And have we been humbled by afflictions? For neither mercies nor afflictions proceed from the dust, but they are the works of our heavenly Father; for it may be that when the tender mercies of God will not allure us, afflictions may drive us to the divine fountain. Let us now cast an eye back for a few years and consider how many hundreds of our nation and how many thousands of other nations have been sent out of time into a never-ending eternity, by the force of the cannon and by the point of the sword. Have we not great cause to think this is the just deserving of our sins; for this is the work of God. Isaiah iii. 11, Woe unto the wicked, it shall be ill with him, for the reward of his hands shall be given him. Here we see that we ought to pray, that God may hasten the time when the people shall beat their swords into plough-shares and their spears into pruning-hooks, and nations shall learn war no more.

And now my dear brethren have we not great reason to be thankful that God in the time of his judgments hath remembered mercy, so that we have the preaching of the Gospel and the use of our bibles, which is the greatest of all mercies; and if after all these advantages we continue in our sins, have we not the greatest reason to fear the judgments of God will be fulfilled on us. He that being often reproved hardneth his neck shall suddenly be destroyed, and that without remedy. Have we not great reason to praise God that he is giving us food and raiment, and to say as David did, Psal. cxxxvii. 1, O give thanks unto the Lord, for his mercy endureth for ever. And now my brethren, when these things make us more humble and more holy, then we may be said to behold the Lamb of God in the sense of the text. And now, in the third place, I am to shew when we may be said not to behold the Lamb of God in the sense of the text: When we are negligent to attend the word of God, and unnecessarily, or are living in any known sin, either of omission or commission, or when we have heard the word preached to us and have not improved that talent put into our hands by a holy life, then we may be said not to behold the Lamb of God in the sense of the text. And now my brethren, I am in the fourth place, to shew how in some things we may be mistaken in beholding the Lamb of God, while we are flattering ourselves with the hopes of salvation on the most slight foundation, because we live in a Christian land and attend to divine service; these things are good in themselves; but there must be a saving change wrought in our hearts, and we must become as new in Christ Jesus; we must not live after the flesh, but after the spirit, for as many as are led by the spirit of God are the sons of God, Rom. viii. 14 and we are to pray that God would keep us from all evil, especially the evil of sin. Bishop Bevrage, in his second Resolution, speaking of sin, he says, "For as God is the centre of all good, so sin is the fountain of all evil in the world, all strife and contention, ignominy and disgrace." Read a little further, and he goes on to protest against sin, "I resolve to hate sin (says he) wherever I find it, whether in myself or in others, in the best of my friends as well as in the worst of my enemies." Here we see my brethren that if we commit any willful sin, either of omission or commission, we become the servants of sin, and are deceiving ourselves, for the apostle hath told us, that the wages of sin is death, Rom. vi 22, 23; but now being made free from sin, and are become the servants of God ye have your fruits into holiness, and in the end eternal life;

for the wages of sin is death, but the gift of God is eternal life through Jesus Christ our Lord. We are to behold the Lamb of God by reading the scriptures, and we must believe that he hath power to give everlasting life. John vi. 47, Verily, verily I say unto you, he that believeth on me hath everlasting life. Do we my brethren believe in the blessed Jesus as we ought? Are we not going the broad way to utter destruction? Are we not leaving the blessed Jesus, who hath the bread of life and is that bread? John vi. 48, I am the bread of life. Here we see that the blessed Jesus hath power to give eternal life to all that come unto him by faith and repentance; and we see that he is calling to us as he did to his disciples, saying, Wilt thou go away also; for this is the language of the scriptures, John vi. 67, 68, Then Simon answered him, lord to whom shall we go? Thou hast the words of eternal life. And we are my brethren to behold the Lamb of God as being the door of eternal life, for this he hath declared in his word to us. John x. 9, I am the door, by me if any man enter he shall be saved, and shall go in and out and find pasture. But it is very plain my brethren that if we come in our sins God will not hear us, but if we come and worship him in spirit and in truth he will have mercy on us. John ix. 31, 32, Now we know that God heareth not sinners, but if any man be a worshipper of God and doth his will, him he heareth. My dear brethren as I am drawing to a conclusion, let me press on you to prepare for death, that great and iresistable king of terrors, by a holy life, and make the word of God the rule of your life; but it may be objected we do not understand the word of God. Mr. Burkit, a great divine of our church says, in the scriptures there is depths that an elephant may swim, and shoals that a lamb may wade. Therefore we must take the plainest text as a key to us. And now my brethren I am in the fifth place to endeavour to rectify any mistake we may labour under, when we are taking on us the form of Godliness, without the power thereof, then we cannot be said to behold the Lamb of God in the sense of the text. We must pray earnestly to God for his holy Spirit to guide us in the way to eternal life; this none can do but God. Let us my brethren lay up treasure in heaven, where neither moth doth corrupt nor thieves break through and steal. Matt. vi. 20-23, Seek first the kingdom of God and his righteousness and all these things shall be added unto you. And now my dear brethren, we must pray earnestly to God for the influence of his holy spirit to guide us through this howling wilderness and sea of trouble to the mansions of glory, and we should pray that God would give us grace to love and to fear him, for if we love God, black as we be, and despised as we are, God will love us. Acts x. 34, Then Peter opened his mouth and said, of a truth I perceive that God has no respect to persons. Ver. 35, In every nation he that feareth him is accepted of him. Psalm. xxxiv. 8, O taste and see that the Lord is good, and blessed is the man that trusteth in him. Ver. 15, The eyes of the Lord are upon the righteous, and his ears are open to their cry. Let us my dear brethren remember that the time is hastening when we shall appear before the Lamb of God to give an account for the deeds done in the body, when we shall be stumbling over the dark mountains of death looking into an endless eternity. O that we may be of that happy number that shall stand with their lamps burning. Matt. xxv. 7, Then all those virgins rose and trimmed their lamps. Come now my brethren, let us examine ourselves whether we have had a saving change wrought in our hearts, and have been brought to bow to the divine sovereignty of the most high God, and to flee to the armies of Jesus, for he is the author of our peace, and the finisher of our faith. Heb. xii. 2, Looking to Jesus the author and finisher of our faith. Come now my brethren, we are one flesh and bone, let us serve the one living and true God. Come let us behold the Lamb of God by an eye of faith for without faith it is impossible to please God. Heb. xi. 5, For faith my brethren is of the things not seen. Let us my brethren strive by the grace of God to become new creatures; for if any man be in Christ he is a new creature, 2. Cor. iv. 17. Let us come to the divine fountain, by constant prayer. Psal. iv. 1, Give ear to my words O Lord, consider my meditations, ver. 2, 3. Let us improve our talents by a holy life, striving to make our calling and election sure, for now is the accepted time; behold now is the day of salvation. 2. Cor. vi. 2. Let us pray that God give us of the waters that the woman of Samaria drank. John xiv. 19, but whosoever shall drink of the water I shall give him shall never thirst, but the water I shall give him shall be in him a well of water springing up into everlasting life. O my dear brethren we should be brought humbly to submit to the will of God at all times, and to say God be merciful to us sinners, Acts iii. 19, Repent and be converted that your sins may be blotted out. My dear brethren we are many of us seeking for a temporal freedom, and I pray that God would grant your desire; if we are slaves it is by the permission of God; If we are free, it must be by the power of the most high God; be not discouraged, but cheerfully perform the duties of the day, sensible that the same power that created the heavens and the earth and causeth the greater light to rule the day and the lesser to rule the night, can cause a universal freedom; and I pray God may give you grace to seek that freedom which tendeth to everlasting life. John viii. 32, And ye shall know the truth, and the truth shall make you free. Ver. 36, If the Son shall make you free, then you shall be free indeed. But as I am advanced to the age of seventy-one years, I do not desire temporal freedom for myself. My brethren, if we desire to be a happy people, we must be a holy people, and endeavour to keep the commandments of God, and we should pray that God would come and knock at the door of our hearts by the power of his holy spirit, and give us a stedfastness in the merits of Christ, and we are to believe in Christ for eternal salvation. Mr. Stoddard, a great divine, says, in speaking of appearing in the righteousness of Christ, when men believe it is part of God's covenant, to make them continue to believe. Job. vi. 12. And again he saith, since God hath promised life unto all that believe in this righteousness, it must needs be safe to appear before God in this righteousness. Jer. iii. 22, Return ye back-sliding children and I will heal your back-slidings; behold we come unto thee for thou art the Lord our God. My dear brethren let not your hearts be set too much on the pleasures of this life; for if it were possible for one man to gain a thousand freedoms, and had not an interest in the merits of Christ, where must all the advantage be; for what would it profit a man if he should gain the whole world and loose his own soul. Matt. xvi. 26. My brethren we know not how soon God may send the cold hand of death to summon us out of this life to a never-ending eternity, there to appear before the judgment seat of Christ. 2 Cor. v. 10, For all must appear before the judgment seat of Christ. And now I conclude with a few words – let me tell you my dear brethren, that in a few days we must all appear before the judgment seat of Christ, there to give an account of the deeds done in the body. Let us my brethren strive to be so prepared for death, by the grace of God. That when the time shall come when we are shaking off the shackles of this life, and are passing through the valley of the shadow of death. O may we then be enabled to say, come Lord Jesus come quickly, for thou art the Lamb of God, in whom my soul delighteth; Then my dear brethren all those which have repented of their sins shall hear this voice, come unto me. Matt. xxv. 34, Then shall the King say unto them on his right hand; come ye blessed of my Father, inherit the kingdom prepared for you from the foundation of the world. But if we do not repent of our sins we must hear this voice, Matt. xxv. 41, Then shall he say also unto them on his left hand, depart from me ye cursed into everlasting fire prepared for the devil and his angels. Then will our souls waft away into an endless eternity, and our bodies lodged in the cold and silent grave, there to remain till Christ's second coming. My brethren, we believe the word of God, we must believe this. 1 Cor. xiii. 41, Behold I shew you a mistery, we shall not all sleep, but we shall be changed in a moment in the twinkling of an eye, at the last trumpet; for the trumpet shall sound and the dead shall be raised, ver. 35, For this corruptible must put on incorruption, and this mortals must put on immortality. And now my brethren, let me persuade you to seek the Lord. Isaiah lv. 6, Seek the Lord while he may be found, and call on him while he is near; ver. 7, Let the wicked forsake his way, and the unrighteous man his thoughts, and let him return unto the Lord, and he will have mercy on him, and to our God and he will abundantly pardon. Therefore not be contented with the form of godliness without the power thereof. Amen.

CHAPTER 13

A DIALOGUE ENTITLED THE KIND MASTER AND THE DUTIFUL SERVANT

Master.
1. Come my servant, follow me,
According to thy place;
And surely God will be with thee,
And send thee heav'nly grace.

Servant
2. Dear Master, I will follow thee,
According to thy word,
And pray that God may be with me,
And save thee in the Lord.

Master.
3. My Servant, lovely is the Lord,
And blest those servants be,
That truly love his holy word,
And thus will follow me.

Servant.
4. Dear Master, that's my whole delight,
Thy pleasure for to do;
As for grace and truth's in sight,
Thus far I'll surely go.

Master.
5. My Servant, grace proceeds from God,
And truth should be with thee;
Whence e'er you find it in his word,
Thus far come follow me.

Servant.
6. Dear Master, now without control
I quickly follow thee;
And pray that God would bless thy soul,
His heav'nly place to see.

Master.
7. My Servant, Heaven is high above,
Yea, higher than the sky:
I pray that God would grant his love,
Come follow me thereby.

Servant.
8. Dear Master, now I'll follow thee,
And trust upon the Lord;
The only safety that I see,
Is Jesus's holy word.

Master.
9. My Servant, follow Jesus now,
Our great victorious King;
Who governs all both high and low,
And searches things within.

Servant.
10. Dear Master, I will follow thee,
When praying to our King;
It is the Lamb I plainly see,
Invites the sinner in.

Master.
11. My Servant, we are sinners all,
But follow after grace;
I pray that God would bless thy soul,
And fill thy heart with grace.

Servant.
12. Dear Master I shall follow then,
The voice of my great King;
As standing on some distant land,
Inviting sinners in.

Master.
13. My servant we must all appear,
And follow then our King;
For sure he'll stand where sinners are,
To take true converts in.

Servant.

14. Dear Master, now if Jesus calls,
And sends his summons in;
We'll follow saints and angels all,
And come into our King.

Master.

15. My servant now come pray to God,
Consider well his call;
Strive to obey his holy word,
That Christ may love us all.

A Line *on the present* war.

Servant

16. Dear Master now it is a time,
A time of great distress;
We'll follow after things divine,
And pray for happiness.

Master.

17. Then will the happy day appear.
That virtue shall increase;
Lay up the sword and drop the spear,
And Nations seek for peace.

Servant.

18. Then shall we see the happy end,
Tho' still in some distress;
That distant foes shall act like friends,
And leave their wickedness.

Master.
19. We pray that God would give us grace,
   And make us humble too;
   Let ev'ry Nation seek for peace,
   And virtue make a show.

Servant.
20. Then we shall see the happy day,
   That virtue is in power;
   Each holy act shall have its sway,
   Extend from shore to shore.

Master.
21. This is the work of God's own hand,
   We see by precepts given;
   To relieve distress and save the land,
   Must be the pow'r of heav'n.

Servant.
22. Now glory be unto our God,
   Let ev'ry nation sing;
   Strive to obey his holy word,
   That Christ may take them in.

Master.
23. Where endless joys shall never cease,
   Blest Angels constant sing;
   The glory of their God increase,
   Hallelujahs to their King.

Servant.
24. Thus the Dialogue shall end,
   Strive to obey the word;
   When ev'ry Nation acts like friends,
   Shall be the sons of God.

25. Believe me now my Christian friends,
Believe your friend call'd Hammon:
You cannot to your God attend,
And serve the God of Mammon.

26. If God is pleased by his own hand
To relieve distresses here;
And grant a peace throughout the the (*sic*)
land,
'Twill be a happy year.

27. 'Tis God alone can give us peace;
It's not the pow'r of man:
When virtuous pow'r shall increase,
'Twill beautify the land.

28. Then shall we rejoice and sing
By pow'r of virtues word,
Come sweet Jesus, heav'nly King,
Thou art the Son of God.

29. When virtue comes in bright array,
Discovers ev'ry sin;
We see the dangers of the day,
And fly unto our King.

30. Now glory be unto our God,
All praise be justly given;
Let ev'ry soul obey his word,
And seek the joy of heav'n.

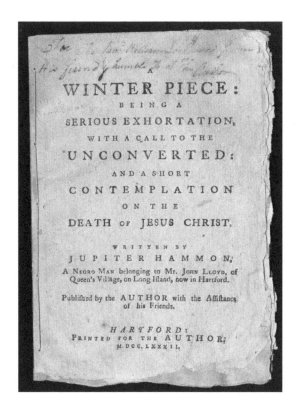

Jupiter Hammon, "A Winter Piece"
Cover page: Connecticut Imprints 1782 H225w,
The Connecticut Historical Society, Used by permission.
Inscribed by Jupiter Hammon to Reverend Lockwood.

CHAPTER 14

A WINTER PIECE;

BEING A SERIOUS EXHORTATION, WITH A CALL TO THE UNCONVERTED; AND A SHORT CONTEMPLATION ON THE DEATH OF JESUS CHRIST, WRITTEN BY JUPITER HAMMON, A Negro Man belonging to Mr. John Lloyd, of Queen's village, on Long Island, now in Hartford.

As I have been desired to write something more than Poetry, I shall endeavour to write from these words, Matthew xi, 28. Come unto me all ye that labour and are heavy laden.

My Brethren, I shall endeavour by divine assistance, to shew what is meant by coming to the Lord Jesus Christ labouring and heavy laden, and to conclude, I shall contemplate on the death of Jesus Christ.

My Brethren, in the first place, I am to shew what is meant by coming to Christ labouring and heavy laden. We are to come with a sense of our own unworthiness, and to confess our sins before the most high God, and to come by prayer and meditation, and we are to confess Christ to be our Saviour and mighty Redeemer. Matthew x, 33. Whosoever shall confess me before men, him will I confess before my heavenly father. Here, my brethren, we have great encouragement to come to the Lord, and ask for the influence of his holy spirit, and that he would give us the water of eternal life, John iv, 14. Whosoever shall drink of this water as the woman of Samaria did, shall never thirst; but it shall be in them a well of water springing up to eternal life, then we shall believe in the merits of Christ, for our eternal salvation, and come labouring and heavy laden with a sense of our lost and undone state without an interest in the merits of Christ. It should be our greatest care to trust in the Lord, as David did, Psalm xxxi, 1. In thee O Lord put I my trust.

My Brethren, we must come to the divine fountain to turn us from sin to holiness, and to give us grace to repent of all our sins; this none can do but God. We must come labouring and heavy laden not trusting to our own righteousness, but we are to be cloathed with the righteousness of Christ. Then may we apply this text, Psalm xxxiii, 7. Blessed be he whose transgressions is forgiven, whose sins is covered. This we must seek for by prayer and meditation, and we are to pray without ceasing, and the word is set forth by David in Psalm lxi, 1. Have mercy on me O God, according to thy loving kindness, according unto the multitude of thy tender mercies blot out may transgressions. My Brethren we are to come poor in spirit.

In the second place in order to come to the divine foundation laboring and heavy laden, we are to avoid all bad company, to keep ourselves pure in heart.

Matthew v. 8. Blessed are the poor in heart for they shall see God. Now, in order to see God we must have a saving change wrought in our hearts, which is the work of god's holy spirit which we are to ask for, Matthew vii, 7. Ask and it shall be given you, seek and ye shall find. It may be asked what shall we find? Ye will find the mercies of God to allure you, the influence of his holy spirit to guide you in the right way to eternal life, Matt. vii, 8. For every one that asketh receiveth, but then my brethren we are to ask in a right manner, with faith and repentance, for except we repent we shall surely die, that is, we must suffer the wrath of the most high God, who will turn you away with this pronunciation depart from me ye workers of iniquity, Matt. vii, 23. Therefore you see how dangerous a thing it is to live in any known sin, either of commission or omission, for if we commit any wilful sin, we become the servants of sin John viii, 34. Whosoever commiteth sin is the servant of sin John viii, 34. Whosoever commiteth sin is the servant of sin. My dear brethren, have we not rendered ourselves too much the servants of sin, by a breach of God's holy commandments, by breaking his holy Sabbath, when we should have been fitting for our great and last change? Have we not been amusing ourselves with the pleasures of this life, or, if we have attended divine service, have we been sincere? For God will not be mocked, for he knows our thoughts. John iv, 24, God is a spirit, and they that worship him must worship him in spirit and in truth. Therefore my Brethren, we see how necessary it is that we should be sincere when we attempt to come to the Lord whether in public service of private devotion, for it is not the outward appearance but sincerity of the heart. This we must manifest by a holy life; for it is not every one that says Lord, Lord, shall enter into the kingdom of Heaven; but he that doth the will of my heavenly Father, Matt. vii, 21.

Therefore, we ought to come laboring and heaven laden to the throne of grace, and pray that God may be pleased to transform us anew in Christ Jesus. But it may be objected by those who have had the advantage of studying, every one is not calculated for teaching of others. To those I answer, Sirs, I do not attempt to teach those who I know are able to teach me, but I shall endeavour by divine assistance to enlighten the minds of my brethren; for we are a poor despised nation, whom God in his wise providence has permitted to be brought from their native place to a christian land, and many thousands born in what are called christian families, and brought up to years of understanding. In answer to the objectors, Sirs, pray given me leave to enquire into the state of those children that are born in those christian families, have they been baptised, taught to read, and learnt their catechism? Surely this is a duty incumbent on masters or heads of families. Sirs, if you had a sick child would you not send for a doctor? If your house was on fire would you not strive to put it out to save your interest? Surely then you ought to use the means appointed to save the souls which God has committed to your charge, and not forget the words of Joshua, as for me and my house we will serve the Lord. Children should be taught the fear of God: See what Solomon says, Prov. viii, 18. The fear of the Lord is to hate evil; chapter ix, 10. the fear of the Lord is the beginning of wisdom; chapter xiv, 17. The fear of the Lord is a fountain of life. Here we see that children should fear the Lord.

But I turn to my Brethren for whom this discourse is designed. My Brethren, if ye are desirous to be saved by the merits of Jesus Christ, ye must forsake all your sins, and come to the Lord by prayer and re-pentance of all your former sins, come labouring and heavy laden; for we are invited to come and rely on the blessed Jesus for eternal salva-tion. Matthew x, 32. Whosoever shall confess me before men, him will I confess before my heavenly father. Here we have our Saviour's words for our encouragement. See to it my brethren that ye live a holy life, and that ye walk more circumspect or holy than ye have done heretofore. I now assure you that God is a spirit, and they that wor-ship him must worship him in spirit and in truth; therefore if ye would come unto him, come as the poor publican did, and say God be mer-ciful to me a sinner: Luke xv, 11. And the publican standing afar off would not lift up so much as his eyes unto heaven, but smote upon his breast saying, God be merciful to me a sinner. For if we hope to be saved by the merits of Jesus Christ, we cast off all self-dependence, as to our own righteousness; for by grace ye are saved through faith, and that not of yourselves, it is the gift of God.

Here we see that the imperfections of human nature is such, that we cannot be saved by any other way but the name of Jesus Christ, and that there must be a principle of love and fear of God implanted in our hearts, if we desire to come to the divine fountain laboring and heavy laden with our sins. But the enquirer may enquire how do you prove this doctrine, are you not imposing on your brethren, as you know many of them cannot read. To this I answer, Sir, I do not mean to im-pose on my brethren, but to shew them there must be a principle of fear and love to God, and now I am to prove this doctrine that we ought to fear God, Psalm ciii, 11. For as the heavens is high above the earth, so great is his mercy towards them that fear him. Verse 13. Like as a father pitieth his children, so the Lord pitieth them that fear him. Psalm xxxiv,

9. O fear the Lord ye his saints, for there is no want to them that fear him. Verse 11. Come ye children hearken unto me, I will teach you the fear of the Lord. This may suffice to prove the doctrine that we ought to fear the Lord, here my brethren we see how much our salvation depends on our being transformed anew in Christ Jesus, for we are sinners by nature and are adding thereunto every day of our life, for man is prone to evil as the sparks to fly upward, this thought should put us on our guard against all manner of evil, especially of bad company. This leads me to say, we should endeavour to glorify God in all our actions whether spiritual or temporal, for the apostle hath told us whatever we do, do all to the glory of God. 1 Cor. x, 30.

Let us now labour for that food which tendeth unto eternal life, this none can give but God only: My Brethren, it is your duty to strive to make your calling and election sure by a holy life, working out your salvation with fear and trembling, for we are invited to come without money and without price.

Isaiah lv, 1 Have every one that thirsteth come ye to the waters, and he that hath no money, come ye buy and eat; yea come and buy wine and milk without money and without trice. This leads me to say if we suffer as sinners, under the light of the gospel as sinners, the fault is in us, for our Saviour hath told us if he had not come we should not had sin, but now they have no cloak for their sins. Let us now improve our talents by coming laboring and burthened with a sense of our sins. This certainly is a necessary duty of all mankind, to come to the divine fountain for mercy and for the influence of God's holy spirit to guide us through this wilderness to the mansions of eternal glory.

My Brethren, have we not great encouragement to come unto the Lord Jesus Christ, Matthew vii, 7. Ask and it shall be given you, knock and it shall be opened unto you. Therefore if ye desire to be saved by the merits of Christ, ye must come as the prodigal son did, Luke xv, 21. And the son said unto him father I have sinned against Heaven and in thy sight, and am no more worthy to be called thy son. This is the language of the true penetent, for he is made sensible that there is no other name given by which he can be saved, but by the name of Jesus. Therefore we should put our trust in him and strive to make our calling and election sure, by prayer and meditation. Psalm lv, 1. Give ear to my prayer O God, and hide not thyself from my supplication.

But, my Brethren, are we not too apt to put off the thoughts of death till we are sick, or some misfortune happens to us, forgetting that bountiful hand who gives us every good gift: Doth not the tokens of mortality call aloud to us all to prepare for death our great and last change, not flattering ourselves with the hopes of a long life, for we know not what a day may bring forth, therefore my Brethren let it be your greatest care to prepare for death, that great and irresistible king of terrors. Are we many of us advanced in years and we know not how soon God may be pleased to call us out of this life to an endless eternity, for this is the lot of all men, once to die, and after that the judgment. Let us now come to the Lord Jesus Christ, with a sense of our own impotency to do any good thing of ourselves, and with a thankful remembrance of the death of Christ who died to save lost man, and hath invited us to come to him laboring and heavy laden. My ancient Brethren, let us examine ourselves now whither we have had a saving change wrought in our hearts, and have repented of our sins, have we made it our greatest care to honor God's holy word and to keep his holy Sabbath's and to obey his commandments.

Exodus xx, 6. And shewing mercy to thousands of them that love me and keep my commandments, have we been brought to bow to the divine sovereignty of the Most High God and to fly to the arms of the crucified Jesus, at whose crucification the mountains trembled, and the rocks rent, and the graves were opened and many bodies of saints that slept arose. Come my dear fellow servants and brothers, Africans by nation, we are all invited to come, Acts x, 34. Then Peter opened his mouth and said, of a truth I perceive that God is no respecter of persons, verse 35, But in every nation he that feareth him is accepted of him. My Brethren, many of us are seeking a temporal freedom, and I wish you may obtain it; remember that all power in heaven and on earth belongs to God; if we are slaves it is by the permission of God, if we are free it must be by the power of the most high God. Stand still and see the salvation of God, cannot that same power that divided the waters from the waters for the children of Israel to pass through, make way for your freedom, and I pray that God would grant your desire, and that he may give you grace to seek that freedom which tendeth to eternal life, John viii, 32, And ye shall know the truth and the truth shall make you free. Verse 36, If the Son shall make you free you shall be free indeed.

This we know my brethren, that all things work together for good to them that love God. Let us manifest this love to God by a holy life.

My dear Brethren, as it hath been reported that I had petitioned to the court of Hartford against freedom, I now solemnly declare that I never have said, nor done any thing, neither directly nor indirectly, to promote or to prevent freedom; but my answer hath always been I am a stranger here and I do not care to be concerned or to meddle with public affairs, and by this declaration I hope my friends will be satisfied, and all prejudice removed. Let us all strive to be united together in love, and to become new creatures, for if any man be in Christ Jesus he is a new creature, 2 Cor. v. 17. Therefore if any man be in Christ he is a new creature Old things are passed away behold all things are become new, now to be a new creature is to have our minds turned from darkness to light, from sin to holiness and to have a desire to serve God with our whole hearts, and to follow his precepts. Psalm xix, 10. More to be desired than gold, yea than much fine gold, sweeter than honey and the honey comb. Verse 11. Moreover by them is thy servant warned, and by keeping them there is great reward.

Let me now, my brethren, persuade you to prepare for death by prayer and meditation, that is the way Mat. vi. But when thou prayest enter into thy closet, and, when thou hast shut the door, pray to thy father in secret, and thy father which seeth in secret shall reward thee openly.

My Brethren, while we continue to sin we are enemies to Christ, ruining ourselves, and a hurt to the commonwealth.

Let us now, my brethren, come laboring and heavy laden with a sense of our sins, and let us pray that God may in his mercy be pleased to lift up the gates of our hearts, and open the doors of our souls, that the King of Glory may come in, and set these things home on our hearts. Psalm xxiv. 7. Lift up your heads O ye gates, and be ye lifted up ye everlasting doors, and the King of Glory shall come in; then may we rely on the merits of Christ, and say, as David did, In the Lord put I my trust, Psalm xi. 4. And again, whom have I in heaven but thee, and there is none on earth I desire besides thee.

And now, my brethren, I shall endeavour to prove that we are not only ruining ourselves by sin, but many others. If the generality of men were more humble and more holy, we should not hear the little children in the street taking God's holy name in vain. Surely our conversation should be yea, yea, and nay, nay, or to that purpose. Matt. v. 7. But let your communication be yea, yea, nay, nay, for whatsoever is more than these cometh of evil. Therefore my Brethren, we should endeavor to walk humble and holy, to avoid the appearance of evil; to live a life void of offence toward God and towards man. Hear what David saith, Psalm i, 1. Blessed is the man that walketh not in the counsel of the ungodly nor standeth in the way of sinners. Here we see how much it becomes us to live as Christians, not in rioting and drunkenness, uncleanness, Sabbath breaking, swearing, taking God's holly name in vain; but our delight should be in the law of the Lord.

The righteous man is compared to a tree that bringeth forth fruit in season. Psalm I, 3. And he shall be like a tree planted by the rivers of water, that bringeth forth fruit in his season: His leaf also shall not wither, and whatsoever he doeth shall prosper. Let us not forget the words of holy David, man is but dust like the flower of the field. Psalm ciii, 15.

Let us remember the uncertainty of human life, and that we are many of us within a step of the grave, hanging only be the single thread of life, and we know not how soon God may send the cold hand of death and cut the thread of life; Then will our souls either ascend up to the eternal mansions of glory or descend down to eternal misery, our bodies lodged in the cold and silent grave, numbered with the dead, then shall the scripture be fulfilled. Gen. iii. 19. In the sweat of thy face shalt thou eat bread, till thou return to the ground, for out of it was thou taken, for dust thou art and to dust thou shalt return.

Now I am to call to the unconverted, my brethren, if we desire to become true converts we must be born again, we must have a spiritual regeneration. John iii, 3. Verity, verily I say unto you, except a man be born again he cannot see the kingdom of God.

My brethren, are we not, many of us, ignorant of this spiritual regeneration? Have we seen our lost and undone condition without an interest in the merits of Jesus Christ; have we come weary and heavy laden with our sins, and to say with holy David, Psalm vi. 10. Lord rebuke me not in thine anger, neither chasten me in thy hot displeasure. Hath it been our great care to prepare for death our great and last change, by prayer and meditation.

My dear brethren, though we are servants and have not so much time as we could wish for, yet we must improve the little time we have.

Mr. Burket, a great divine of our church, says, a man's hand may be on his plow and his heart in heaven, by putting up such prayers and ejaculations as these, Psalm lxi. 1. Hear my cry O God, attend to my prayer, and again, Whom have I in heaven but thee, and there is none on earth I desire besides thee.

We should pray that God would give us his holy spirit, that we may not be lead into temptation, and that we may be delivered from evil, especially the evil of sin. Rom. vi. 22, 23. But now, being made free from sin, and become servants of God, ye have your fruit unto holiness, and the end everlasting life. For the wages of sin is death, but the gift of God is eternal life through Jesus Christ our Lord.

My brethren, seeing I am desired by my friends to write something more than poetry, give me leave to speak plainly to you. Except you repent and forsake your sins ye must surely die. Now we see how much it becomes us to break our alliance with sin and Satan, and to fly to a crucified Saviour, and to enlist under Christ's banner, and that he may give us grace to become his faithful subjects, should be our constant prayers. We should guard against every sin, especially bad language.

Therefore, my Brethren, we should always be guarding against every evil word, for we are told that the tongue is an evil member, for with the tongue we bless God, and with the tongue we curse men. 1 Peter iii. 10. For he that loves life, and would see good days, let him refrain his tongue from evil and his lips from speaking guile. But the thoughtless and unconverted sinner is going on in open rebellion, against that divine power which can in one minute cut the thread of life, and cast them away with this pronunciation, Depart from me ye workers of iniquity. Matt. xxv. 41. Then shall he say also unto them on the left hand, depart from me ye cursed into everlasting fire prepared for the devil and his angels.

And now, my brethren, shall we abuse the divine sovereignty of a holy God, who hath created us rational creatures, capable of serving him under the light of the Gospel, for he hath told us if he had not come unto us we had not had sin, but now we have no cloak for our sin.

Come now my dear brethren, accept of Jesus Christ on the terms of the gospel, which is by faith and repentance. Come laboring and heaven laden with your sins, and a sense of your unworthiness.

My Brethren, it is not we servants only that are unworthy, but all mankind by the fall of Adam, became guilty in the sight of God. Gen. ii. 17. Surely then we are sinners by nature, and are daily adding thereto by evil practices, and it is only by the merits of Jesus Christ we can be saved, we are told that he is a Jew that is a Jew in his heart, so he is a Christian that is a Christian in his heart, and it is not every one that says Lord, Lord, shall enter into the kingdom of God, but he that doth the will of God. Let our superiors act as they shall think it best, we must resolve to walk in the steps our Saviour hath set before us which was a holy life, a humble submission to the will of God. Luke xxii. 41, 42. And he was withdrawn from them about a stones cast, and he kneeled down and prayed saying, father if thou be willing remove this cup from me, nevertheless not my will but thine be done.

Here we have the example our Saviour who came down from heaven to save mankind, lost and undone without an interest in the merits of Jesus Christ, the blessed Jesus then gave his life a ransom for all that come unto him by faith and repentance; and shall not he that spared not his own son, but delivered him up for us all, with him freely give all things.

Come let us seek first, Christ, the kingdom of God; and his righteousness, all other things shall be added unto you. Matt. vi. 33. Here we have great encouragement to come to the divine fountain.

Bishop Beverage says, in his third resolution, the eyes to the Lord is intent upon us, he seeth our actions; if our sins are not washed out with our tears, and crost with the blood of Christ, we cannot be saved. Come my brethren, O taste and see that the Lord is good, and blessed is the man that trusteth in him. Psalm xxxiv. 8. Let us not stand as Felix did, and say, almost thou persuadest me to be a Christian, but, let us strive to be altogether so. If ye desire to become converts you must have a saving change wrought in your hearts that shall bring forth good works, meet for repentance: Acts iii. 19. Repent ye therefore, be converted: We are not to trust in our own strength but to trust in the Lord; Proverbs iii, 4. "Trust in the Lord with all thine heart, and lean not unto thine own understanding."

My brethren, are we not encircled with many temptations, the flesh, the world and the devil; these must be resisted at all times. We must see to it that we do not grieve the holy spirit of God. Come let us my dear brethren, draw near to the Lord by faith and repentance, for faith without works is dead. James ii. 20. And Rom. x, 10. For with the heart man believeth, and with the mouth confession is made unto salvation. Here we see there is something to be done by us as Christians; therefore we should walk worthy of our profession, not forgetting that there is a divine power which takes a just survey of all our actions, and will reward every one according to their works. Psalm lxii, 2. "Also unto the Lord belongeth mercy, for thou rememberest every man according to his works." Therefore it is our indispensable duty to improve all opportunities to serve God, who gave us his only son to save all that come unto him by faith and repentance.

Let me, my brethren, persuade you to a serious consideration of your danger while you continue in an unconverted state. Did you feel the operations of God's holy spirit, you then would leave all for an interest in the merits of Christ; "For the kingdom of heaven is like a treasure hid in a field; for which a man will sell all that he hath to purchase, Matt. x. 44." So will every true penitent part with all for the sake of Christ. I shall not attempt to drive you to Christ by the terrors of the law, but I shall endeavour to allure you by the invitation of the gospel, to come laboring and heavy laden.

Matt. xi. 27. Man at his best estate is like a shadow of the field. We should always be preparing for death, not having our hearts set on the things of this life: For what profit will it be to us, to gain the whole world and loose his own soul. Matt. xvi. 26. We should be always preparing for the will of God, working out our salvation with fear and trembling. O may we abound in the works of the Lord. Let us not stand as fruitless trees or cumberers of the ground, for by your works you shall be justified. And by your works you shall be condemned; for every man shall be rewarded according to his works, Matt. xvi. 27. Let us then be pressing forward to the mark, for the prize of the high calling of God in Christ Jesus. Let our hearts be fixed where true joys are to be found. Let us lay up treasures in Heaven, where neither moth nor rust doth corrupt, nor thieves break through nor steal. Matt. vi. 20.

Now I am come to contemplate the death of Christ, it remains I make a short contemplation. The death of Christ who died! Died to save lost man, 1 Cor. xv. 21. "For since by man came death, by man came also the resurrection from the dead: For as in Adam all died even so in Christ, shall all be made alive." Let us turn to the scriptures, and there we shall see how our Saviour was denied by one and betrayed by another. Matt. xxvi, 14. Judas went unto the Chief Priest, and said, what will you give me, and they agreed for thirty pieces of silver, then they sought opportunity to betray him. Verse 28. For this is my blood of the New Testament, which is shed for many for the remission of sins. Ver. 33. Peter answered and said unto him, though all men should be offended because of thee, yet will I never be offended. Ver 34. Jesus said unto him, verily I say unto thee, this night before the cock crow, thou shalt deny me thrice. Ver. 38, Then saith he unto them, my soul is exceeding sorrowful, even unto death: tarry ye here and watch with me. Ver. 39. And he went a little further and fell on his face and prayed, saying, O Father, if it be possible, let this cup pass from me: Nevertheless not as I will, but as thou wilt.

My Brethren, here we see the love of God plainly set before us; that while we were yet sinners, he sent his son to die for all those that come unto him laboring and heavy laden with a sense of their sins; let us come with a thankful remembrance of his death, whose blood was shed for us guilty worms of the dust. Matt. xxvi. 63. But Jesus held his peace, and the High Priest answered and said unto him, I adjure thee by the Living God, that thou tell us, whether thou be the Christ the son of God. And ver. 64. Jesus saith unto him, thou hast said: nevertheless I say unto you, hereafter shall ye see the Son of Man sitting on the right hand of power, and coming in the clouds of heaven. Ver. 64. Then the High Priest rent his clothes, saying, he hath spoken blasphemy; what further need have we of witness: Behold, now ye have heard his blasphemy. Here the High Priest charged the blessed Jesus with blasphemy: but we must believe that he is able to save all that come unto him, by faith and repentance. Matt. xxviii. 18. And Jesus came and spoke unto them, saying, all power is given unto me in heaven and on earth. As this should excite us to love and fear God, and to strive to keep his holy commandments, which is the only rule of life: But how apt are we to forget that God spoke these words, saying, I am the Lord thy God, which brought thee out of the land of Egypt and out of the house of bondage, Exod. xx. 1. Thus we see how the children of Israel were delivered from the Egyptian service.

But my Brethren, we are invited to the blessed Jesus, who was betrayed by one and denied by another. Matt. xx. 24. The Son of Man goeth as it is written of him; but woe unto that man by whom the Son of Man is betrayed; it had been good for that man if he had never been born. Ver. 24. Then Judas which betrayed him answered and said, Master is it I? He said unto him, thou hast said.

Thus we see, my Brethren, that there is a woe pronounced against every one that sins by omission or commission, are we not going on in our sins, and disobeying the word of God: "If ye love me, ye will keep my commandments." Are we not denying the Lord Jesus, as Peter did. Matt xxvi. 14. Then began he to curse and swear, saying, I know not the man; and immediately the cock crew. And ver. 74. And Peter remembered the words of Jesus, which he said unto him, before the cock crow thou shalt deny me thrice: And he went out and wept bitterly. Surely then we ought to come to the Divine Sovereign, the blessed Jesus who was crucified for us sinners. Oh! We ought to come on the bended knees of our souls, and say, Lord, we believe, help thou our unbelief. Come my Brethren, let us cry to the life giving Jesus, and say, Son of God, have mercy on us! Lamb of God, that taketh away the sins of the world, have mercy on us! Let us cast off all self-dependence, and rely on a crucified Saviour. Luke xxiii. 20. Pilate therefore, willing to release Jesus, spoke again to them. Ver. 21. But they cried, saying, crucify him. Here we may see the love of God, in giving his Son to save all that come unto him by faith and repentance. Let us trace the sufferings of our Saviour a little further: Matt. xxvi. 42. He went away again the second time, and prayed, saying, O my Father, if this cup may not pass away from me, except I drink it, thy will be done. Here we trace our Saviour's example set before us; so that we should not murmur at the hand of Divine Providence; for God hath a right to deal with his creatures as he pleaseth.

Come let us contemplate on the death of the blessed Jesus; and on the fearful judgment of the Lord passing on the guilty sinner. Luke xxiii. 30. Then shall they begin to say to the mountains, fall on us, and to the hills, cover us. Ver. 32, 33. And there were also two malefactors led with him to be put to death; and when they were come to the place, which is called Calvary, there they crucified him and the malefactors, one of the right hand, and the other on the left; and thus was the scripture fulfilled; For he was numbered with transgressors. Matt. xxvii. 29. And when they had plated a crown of thorns, they put it upon his head, and a reed in his right hand. Ver. 41, 42. Likewise the Chief Priests mocking him, with the Scribes and elders, said, he saved others, himself he cannot save: If he be the king of Israel, let him come down from the cross, and we will believe him. Ver. 44. Now from the sixth hour there was darkness over all the land unto the ninth hour. Ver. 46. And about the ninth hour Jesus cried with a loud voice, saying, Eli, Eli, Lama Sabachthani! That is to say, my God, my God, why hast thou forsaken me?

My brethren, should not a sense of these things on our mind implant in us a spirit of love to God, which hath provided a Saviour, who is able to save to the uttermost all that come unto him by faith and repentance. 2. Cor. vii. 10. For Godly sorrow worketh repentance to salvation, not to be repented of, but the sorrow of the world worketh death. My brethren, see what sin hath done; it hath made all flesh guilty in the sight of God.

May we not adopt the language of David. Psalm. lxxix 8. O remember not against us former iniquities. Let thy tender mercies speedily present us. Turn us again, O Lord, God of Iosts, cause thy face to shine, and we shall be saved.

Let us contemplate a little further on the death of Christ. Matt. xxvii. 40. Jesus, when he had cried with a loud voice, yielded up the ghost. Ver. 4, And behold the vail of the temple was rent in twain, from the top to the bottom; and the earth did quake, and the rocks rent. Here we see that the death of Christ caused all nature to tremble, and the power of heaven shaken: Here we may see not only the evil of sin, but also the unmeritted mercy of God, in giving his only Son. Should not our hearts be filled with fear and love to God; and we must believe that Jesus is the Son of God. Matt. xxvii. 54. Now when the Centurion and they that were with him, watching Jesus saw the earth quake, and those things that were done, they feared greatly, saying, truly this was the Son of God. Now this was done for the remission of our sins, for without shedding of blood there is no remission of sin. This we have confirmed in the holy sacrament. Matt. xxvi. 27. For this is my blood of the New Testament, which was shed for many: But the unbelieving Jews still persisted in their unbelief, and would have prevented the resurrection of our Saviour, if it had been in their power. Matt. xxvii. 62. The Chief Priests and Pharisees come together unto Pilate. Ver. 63, Saying, Sir, we remember that that deceiver said, while he was yet alive, after three days I will rise again. Ver. 66. So they went and made the sepulcher sure, sealing the stone and setting a watch. Here we see the spirit of unbelief in Nathaniel. John i. 45 and 46. Philip findeth Nathaniel, and saith unto him, we have found him, of whom Moses in the law of the prophets did write, Jesus of Nazareth, the son of Joseph: And Nathaniel said unto him, can there any good thing come out of Nazareth? Philip saith unto him, come and see. Thus we are to come and see the mercy of God, in sending his Son to save lost men. Let us contemplate on the manner of Christ's resurrection. Matt. xxv. 2. Behold there was a great earthquake; for the angel of the Lord descended from heaven, and come and rolled the stone from the door, and sat upon it. Here we see that our Saviour was attended by an angel; one of those holy spirits we read of in the Revelations, vi. 8. They rest not day and night, saying, holy, holy, holy Lord God Almighty, which was and is and is to come. Ver. 4, 12. Saying, with a loud voice, worthy is the Lamb, that was slain, to receive power and riches, and wisdom, and strength, and honor, and glory, and blessing. And our Saviour himself tells us he hath received his power. Matt. xxviii 19. And Jesus came and spoke unto them, saying, all power is given unto me in heaven and in earth. Then he gives his disciples their charge. Ver. 19. Go ye, therefore, and teach all nations, baptizing them in the name of the Father, of the Son, and of the Holy Ghost. But I must conclude in a few words, and say,

My dear Brethren, should we not admire the free grace of God, that he is inviting of us to come and accept of Jesus Christ, on the terms of the gospel; and he is calling us to repent of all our sins: This we cannot do of ourselves, but we must be saved in the use of means not to neglect those two great articles of the Christian religion, baptism and the sacrament; and we ought all of us to seek by prayers: But the scripture hath told us, that we must not depend on the use of means alone. 1ˢᵗ Cor. iii. 6. The apostle says, I have planted Apolos watered, but God gave the increase. Here we see if we are saved, it must be by the power of God's holy spirit. But my dear Brethren the time is hastening when we must appear.

Hartford; Printed for the Author, MDCCLXXXII (1782)

CHAPTER 15

A POEM FOR CHILDREN WITH THOUGHTS ON DEATH

I

O Ye young and thoughtless youth,
Come seek the living God,
The scriptures are a sacred truth,
Ye must believe the word.

Eccle. xii. 1.

II

'Tis God alone can make you wise,
His wisdom's from above,
He fills the soul with sweet supplies
by his redeeming love.   *Prov.* iv. 7.

III

Remember youth the time is short,
Improve the present day
And pray that God may guide your thoughts,
and teach your lips to pray.   *Psalm* xxx. 9.

IV

To pray unto the most high God,
and beg restraining grace,
Then by the power of his word
You'l see the Saviour's face.

V

Little children they may die,
Turn to their native dust,
Their souls shall leap beyond the skies,
And live among the just.

VI

Like little worms they turn and crawl,
and gasp for every breath.
The Blessed Jesus sends his call,
and takes them to his rest.

VII

Thus the youth are born to die,
The time is hastening on,
The Blessed Jesus rends the sky,
and makes his power known.

Psalm ciii. 15.

VIII

Then ye shall hear the angels sing
The trumpet give a sound,
Glory, glory to our King,
The Saviour's coming down.

Matth. xxvi. 64.

IX

Start ye saints from dusty beds
and hear a Saviour call,
Twas Jesus Christ that died and bled,
and thus preserv'd thy soul.

X

This the portion of the just,
Who lov'd to serve the Lord,
Their bodies starting from the dust,
Shall rest upon their God.

XI

They shall join that holy word,
That angels constant sing,
Glory, glory to the Lord,
Hallelujahs to our King.

XII

Thus the Saviour will appear,
With guards of heavenly host,
Those blessed Saints, shall then declare,
Tis Father, Son and Holy Ghost.

Rev. i. 7, 8.

XIII

Then shall ye hear the trumpet sound,
The graves give up their dead,
Those blessed saints shall quick awake,
and leave their dusty beds.

Matth. xxvii. 51, 52.

XIV

Then shall you hear the trumpet sound,
and rend the native sky,
Those bodies starting from the ground,
In the twinkling of an eye.

I Cor. xv. 51, 52, 53, 54

XV

There to sing the praise of God,
and join the angelic train,
And by the power of his word,
unite together again.

XVI

Where angels stand for to admit
Their souls at the first word,
Cast sceptres down at Jesus feet
Crying holy holy Lord.

XVII

Now glory be unto our God
all praise be justly given,
Ye humble souls that love the Lord
Come seek the joys of Heaven.

Hartford, January 1, 1782.

An Essay on Slavery, with submission to Divine
providence, knowing that God Rules over all things —
Written by Jupiter Hammon

Our forefathers came from Africa
Tost over the raging main
To a Christian Shore there for to stay
And not return again.

2
Dark and dismal was the Day
When Slavery began
All humble thoughts were put away
Then slaves were made by Man.

3
When God doth please for to permit
That Slavery should be
It is our Duty to submit
Till Christ shall make us free

4
Come let us join with one consent
With humble hearts and say
For every sin we must repent
And walk in wisdoms way.

5
If we are free we'll pray to God
If we are slaves the same
We firmly fixt in his word
Ye shall not pray in vain.

6
Come blessed Jesus in thy Love
And hear thy Children cry
And send them smiles now from above
And grant them Liberty.

7
Tis thou alone can make us free
We are thy subjects too
Pray give us grace to bend a knee
The time we stay below.

8
Tis unto thee we look for all
Thou art our only King
Thou hast the power to save the soul
And bring us flocking in.

An Essay on Slavery, with submission to Divine
providence, knowing that God Rules over all things,
by Jupiter Hammon, November 10, 1786. First page.
Essay on Slavery: Hillhouse Family Papers (MS 282),
Manuscript and Archives, Yale University Library

CHAPTER 16

AN ESSAY ON SLAVERY,

with Submission to Divine Providence,
that God Rules over all Things.

Written by Jupiter Hammon

1
Our forefathers came from Africa
Tost over the raging main
To a Christian shore there for to stay
And not return again.

2
Dark and dismal was the Day
When slavery began
All humble thoughts were put away
Then slaves were made by Man.

3
When God doth please for to permit
That slavery should be
It is our duty to submit
Till Christ shall make us free

4

Come let us join with one consent
With humble hearts and say
For every sin we must repent
And walk in wisdom's way.

5

If we are free we'll pray to God
If we are slaves the same
It's firmly fixt in his [holy] word
Ye shall not pray in vain.

6

Come blessed Jesus in thy Love
And hear thy children cry
And send them smiles now from above
And grant them Liberty.

7

Tis thou alone can make us free
We are thy subjects too
Pray give us grace to bend a knee
The time we stay below.

8

Tis unto thee we look for all
Thou art our only King
Thou hast the power to save the soul
And bring us flocking in.

9

We come as sinners unto thee
We know thou hast the word
Come blessed Jesus make us free
And bring us to our God.

10

Although we are in Slavery
We will pray unto our God
He hath mercy beyond the sky
Tis in his holy word.

11

Come unto me ye humble souls
Although you live in strife
I keep alive and save the soul
And give eternal life.

12

To all that do repent of sin
Be they bond or free
I am their saviour and their king
They must come unto me.

13

Hear the words now of the Lord
The call is loud and certain
We must be judged by his word
Without respect of person.

14

Come let us seek his precepts now
And love his holy word
With humble soul we'll surely bow
And wait the great reward.

15

Although we came from Africa
We look unto our God
To help our hearts to sigh and pray
And Love his holy word.

16

Although we are in slavery
Bound by the yoke of Man
We must always have a single eye
And do the best we can.

17

Come let us join with humble voice
Now on the christian shore
If we will have our only choice
Tis slavery no more.

18

Now [?] let us not repine
And say his wheels are slow
He can fill our hearts with things divine
And give us freedom too.

19

He hath the power all in his hand
And all he doth is right
And if we are tide [sic] to the yoke of man
We'll pray with all might.

20

This the state of thousands now
Who are on the christian shore
Forget the Lord to whom we bow
And think of him no more.

21

When shall we hear the joyfull sound
Echo the christian shore
Each humble voice with songs resound
That slavery is no more.

22

Then shall we rejoice and sing
Loud praises to our God
Come sweet Jesus heavenly king
The art the son Our Lord.

23

We are thy children blessed Lord
Tho still in slavery
We'll seek thy precepts Love thy word
Untill the day we Die.

24

Come blessed Jesus hear us now
And teach our hearts to pray
And seek the Lord to whom we bow
Before tribunal day.

25

Now glory be unto our God
All praise be justly given
Come seek his precepts love his works
That is the way to Heaven.

Composed by Jupiter Hammon
A Negro Man belonging to Mr John Lloyd
Queens Village on Long Island
November 10th 1786

CHAPTER 17

AN ADDRESS TO THE NEGROES OF THE STATE OF NEW-YORK

WHEN I AM writing to you with a design to say something to you for your good, and with a view to promote your happiness, I can with truth and sincerity join with the apostle Paul, when speaking of his own nation the Jews, and say: "That I have great heaviness and continual sorrow in my heart for my brethren, my kinsmen according to the flesh." Yes my dear brethren, when I think of you, which is very often, and of the poor, despised and miserable state you are in, as to the things of this world, and when I think of your ignorance and stupidity, and the great wickedness of the most of you, I am pained to the heart. It is at times, almost too much for human nature to bear, and I am obliged to turn my thoughts from the subject or endeavour to still my mind, by considering that it is permitted thus to be, by that God who governs all things, who setteth up one and pulleth down another. While I have been thinking on this subject, I have frequently had great struggles in my own mind, and have been at a loss to know what to do. I have wanted exceedingly to say something to you, to call upon you with the tenderness of a father and friend, and to give you the last, and I may say dying advice, of an old man, who wishes your best good in this world, and in the world to come. But while I have had such desires, a sense of my own ignorance, and unfitness to teach others, has frequently discouraged me from attempting to say any thing to you; yet when I thought of your situation, I could not rest easy.

When I was at Hartford in Connecticut, where I lived during the war, I published several pieces which were well received, not only by those of my own colour, but by a number of the white people, who thought they might do good among their servants. This is one consideration, among others, that emboldens me now to publish what I have written to you. Another is, I think you will be more likely to listen to what is said, when you know it comes from a negro, one of your own nation and colour, and therefore can have no interest in deceiving you, or in saying any thing to you, but what he really thinks is your interest, and duty to comply with. My age, I think, gives me some right to speak to you, and reason to expect you will hearken to my advice. I am now upwards of seventy years old, and cannot expect, though I am well, and able to do almost any kind of business, to live much longer. I have passed the common bounds set for man, and must soon go the way of all the earth. I have had more experience in the world than most of you, and I have seen a great deal of the vanity and wickedness of it, I have great reason to be thankful that my lot has been so much better than most slaves have had. I suppose I have had more advantages and privileges than most of you, who are slaves, have ever known, and I believe more than many white people have enjoyed, for which I desire to bless God, and pray that he may bless those who have given them to me. I do not, my dear friends, say these things about myself, to make you think that I am wiser or better than others; but that you might hearken, without prejudice to what I have to say to you on the following particulars.

1st. Respecting obedience to masters. Now whether it is right and lawful, in the sight of God, for them to make slaves of us or not. I am certain that while we are slaves, it is our duty to obey our masters, in all their lawful commands, and mind them unless we are bid to do that which we know to be sin, or forbidden in God's word. The apostle Paul says: "Servants be obedient to them that are your masters according to the flesh, with fear and trembling in singleness in your heart as unto Christ: Not with eye service, as men pleasers, but as the servants of Christ doing the will of God from the heart: With good will doing service to the Lord, and not to men: Knowing that whatever thing as man doeth the same shall he receive of the Lord, whether he be bond or free." –Here is a plain command of God for us to obey our masters. It may seem hard for us, if we think our masters wrong in holding us slaves, to obey in all things, but who of us dare dispute with God! He has commanded us to obey, and we ought to do it cheerfully, and freely. This should be done by us, not only because God commands, but because our own peace and comfort depend upon it. As we depend upon our masters, for what we eat and drink and wear, and for all our comfortable things in this world, we cannot be happy, unless we please them. This we cannot do without obeying them freely, without muttering or finding fault. If a servant strives to please his master and studies and takes pains to do it, I believe there are but few masters who would use such a servant cruelly. Good servants frequently make good masters. If your master is really hard, unreasonable and cruel, there is no way so likely for you to convince him of it, as always to obey his commands, and try to serve him, and take care of his interest, and try to promote it all in your power. If you are proud and stubborn and always finding fault, your master will think the fault lies wholly of your side; but if you are humble, and meek, and bear all things patiently, your master may think he is wrong; if he does not, his neighbours will be apt to see it, and will befriend you, and try to alter his conduct. If this does not do, you must cry to him, who has the hearts of all men in his hands, and turneth them as the rivers of waters are turned.

2nd. The particular I would mention, is honesty and faithfulness.

You must suffer me now to deal plainly with you, my dear brethren, for I do not mean to flatter or omit speaking the truth, whether it is for you, or against you. How many of you are there, who allow yourselves in stealing from your masters. It is very wicked for you not to take care of your masters' goods; but how much worse is it to pilfer and steal from them, whenever you think you shall not be found out. This you must know is very wicked and provoking to God. There are none of you so ignorant but that you must know that this is wrong. Though you may try to excuse yourselves by saying that your masters are unjust to you and though you may try to quiet your consciences in this way, yet if you are honest in owning the truth, you must think it is as wicked, and on some accounts more wicked to steal from your masters, than from others.

We cannot certainly have any excuse, either for taking any thing that belongs to our masters, without their leave, or for being unfaithful in their business. It is our duty to be faithful, not with eye service as men pleasers. We have no right to stay, when we are sent on errands, any longer than to do the business we were sent upon. All the time spent idly is spent wickedly, and is unfaithfulness to our masters. In these things I must say, that I think many of you are guilty. I know that many of you endeavour to excuse yourselves, and say that you have nothing that you can call your own, and that you are under great temptations to be unfaithful and take from your masters. But this will not do; God will certainly punish you for stealing, and for being unfaithful. All that we have to mind, is our own duty. If God has put us in bad circumstances, that is not our fault, and he will not punish us for it. If any are wicked in keeping us so, we cannot help it; they must answer to God for it. Nothing will serve as an excuse to us for not doing our duty. The same God will judge both them and us. Pray then, my dear friends, fear to offend in this way, but be faithful to God, to your masters, and to your own souls.

The next thing I would mention and warn you against, is profaneness. This you know is forbidden by God. Christ tells us, "Swear not at all," and again it is said, "Thou shalt not take the name of the Lord thy God in vain, for the Lord will not hold him guiltless that taketh his name in vain." Now, though the great God has forbidden it, yet how dreadfully profane are many, and I don't know but I may say the most of you! How common it it to hear you take the terrible and awful name of the great God in vain! –To swear by it, and by Jesus Christ, his Son. –How common is it to hear you wish damnation to your companions, and to your own souls –and to sport with, in the name of Heaven and Hell, as if there were no such places for you to hope for or to fear. Oh my friends, be warned to forsake this dreadful sin of profaneness. Pray, my dear friend , believe and realize that there is a God – that he is great and terrible beyond what you can think – that he keeps you in life every moment –and that he can send you to that awful Hell that you laugh at, in an instant, and confine you there for ever; and that he will certainly do it, if you do not repent. You certainly do not believe that there is a God, or that there is a Heaven or Hell, or you would never trifle with them. It would make you shudder, if you hear others do it. If you believe them as much as you believe any thing you see with your bodily eyes.

I have heard some learned and good men say that the heathen, and all that worshipped false gods, never spoke lightly or irreverently of their gods; they never took their names in vain, or jested with those things which they held sacred. Now, why should the true God, who made all things, be treated worse in this respect than those false gods that were made of wood and stone? I believe it is because Satan tempts men to do it. He tried to make them love their false gods. And to speak well of them; but he wishes to have man think lightly of the true God, to take his holy name in vain, and to scoff at and make a jest of all things that are really good. You may think that Satan has not power to do so much, and have so great influence on the minds of men: But the Scripture says, "He goeth about like a roaring Lion, seeking whom he may devour – That he is the prince of the power of the air – and that he rules in the hearts of the children of disobedience, --- and that wicked men are led captive by him, to do his will." All those of you who are profane are serving the devil. You are doing what he tempts and desires you to do. If you could see him with your bodily eyes, would you like to make an agreement with him to serve him, and do as he bid you? I believe most of you would be shocked at this; but you may be certain that all of you who allow yourselves in this sin, are as really serving him and to just as good purpose, as if you met him and promised to dishonor God, and serve him with all your might. Do you believe this? It is true whether you believe it or not. Some of you to excuse yourselves, may plead the example of others, and say that you hear a great many white people, who know more than such poor ignorant Negroes as you are, and some who are rich and great gentlemen, swear, and talk profanely; and some of you may say this of your masters, and say no more than is true. But all this is not a sufficient excuse for you. You know that murder is wicked. If you saw your master kill a man, do you suppose this would be any excuse for you, if you should commit the same crime? You must know it would not; nor will your hearing him curse and swear, and take the name of God in vain, or any other man, be he ever so great or rich, excuse you. God is greater than all other beings, and him we are bound to obey. To him we must give an account for every *idle* word that we speak. He will bring us all, rich and poor, white and black, to his judgment seat. If we are found among those who *feared his name,* and *trembled at his word,* we shall be called good and faithful servants. Our slavery will be at an end, and though ever so mean, low and despised in this world, we shall sit with God in his kingdom, as Kings and Priests, and rejoice for ever and ever. Do not then, my dear friends, take God's holy name in vain, or speak profanely in any way. Let not the example of others lead you into the sin, but reverence and fear that great *and fearful name, the Lord our God.*

I might now caution you against other sins to which you are exposed; but as I meant only to mention those you were exposed to, more than others, by your being slaves, I will conclude what I have to say to you, by advising you to become religious, and to make religion the great business of your lives.

Now I acknowledge that liberty is a great thing, and worth seeking for, if we can get it honestly; and by our good conduct prevail on our masters to set us free: though for my own part I do not wish to be free, yet I should be glad if others, especially the young Negroes, were to be free; for many of us who are grown up slaves, and have always had masters to take care of us, should hardly know how to take care of ourselves; and it may be more for our own comfort to remain as we are. That liberty is a great thing we may know from our own feelings, and we may likewise judge so from the conduct of the white people in the late war. How much money has been spent, and how many lives have been lost to defend their liberty! I must say that I have hoped that God would open their eyes, when they were so much engaged for liberty, to think of the state of the poor blacks, and to pity us. He has done it in some measure, and has raised us up many friends; for which we have reason to be thankful, and to hope in his mercy. What may be done further, he only knows, for *known unto God are all his ways from the beginning*. But this , my dear brethren, is by no means the greatest thing we have to be concerned about. Getting our liberty in this world is nothing to our having the liberty of the children of God. Now the Bible tells us that we are all, by nature, sinners; that we are slaves to sin and Satan, and that unless we are converted, or born again, we must be miserable for ever. Christ says, except a man be born again, he cannot see the kingdom of God; and all that do not see the kingdom of God, must be in the kingdom of darkness. There are but two places where all go after death, white and black, rich and poor; those places are Heaven and Hell. Heaven is a place made for those who are born again, and if you love God; and it is a place where they will be happy for ever. Hell is a place made for those who hate God, and are his enemies, and where they will be miserable to all eternity. Now you may think you are not enemies to God, and do not hate him: but if your heart has not been changed, and you have not become true Christians, you certainly are enemies to God, and have been opposed to him ever since you were born. Many of you, I suppose, never think of this, and are almost as ignorant as the beasts that perish. Those of you who can read, I must beg you to read the Bible; and when ever you can get time, study the Bible; and if you can get no other time, spare some of your time from sleep, and learn what the mind and will of God is. But what shall I say to them who cannot read? This lay with great weight on my mind, when I thought of writing to my poor brethren; but I hope that those who can read will take pity on them, and read what I have to say to them. In hopes of this, I will beg of you to spare no pains in trying to learn to read. If you are once engaged, you may learn. Let all the time you can get be spent in trying to learn to read. Get those who can read, to learn you; but remember, that what you learn for, is to read the Bible. If there was no Bible, it would be no matter whether you could read or not. Reading other books would do you no good. But the Bible is the word of God, and tells you what you must do to please God; it tells you how you may escape misery, and be happy for ever. If you see most people neglect the Bible, and many that can read never look into it, let it not harden you, and make you think lightly of it, and that it is a book of no worth. All those who are really good love the Bible, and meditate on it day and night. In the Bible god has told us every thing it is necessary we should know, in order to be happy here and hereafter. The Bible is a revelation of the mind and will of God to men. Therein we may learn what God is. That he made all things by the power of his work; and that he made all things for his own glory, and not for our glory. That he is over all, and above all his creatures, and more above them than we can think or conceive – that they can do nothing without him – that he upholds them all, and will overrule all things for his own glory. In the Bible likewise we are told what man is. That he was at first made holy, in the image of God; that he fell from that state of holiness, and became an enemy to God; and that since the fall, *all the imaginations of the thoughts of his heart are evil, and only evil, and that continually. That the carnal mind is not subject to the law of God, neither indeed can be.* And that all mankind were under the wrath and curse of God, and must have been for ever miserable, if they had been left to suffer what their sins deserved. It tells us that God, to save some of mankind, sent his Son into this world to die, in the room and stead of sinners; and that now God can save from eternal misery all that believe in his Son, and take him for their Saviour; and that all are called upon to repent, and believe in

Jesus Christ. It tells us that those who do repent and believe, and are friends to Christ, shall have many trials and sufferings in this world, but that they shall be happy for ever, after death, and reign with Christ to all eternity. The Bible tells us that this world is a place of trial, and that there is no other time or place for us to alter, but in this life. If we are Christians when we die, we shall awake to the resurrection of life; if not, we shall awake to the resurrection of damnation. It tells us we must all live in Heaven or Hell, be happy or miserable, and that without end. The Bible does not tell us of but two places, for all to go to. There is no place for innocent folks, that are not Christians. There is no place for ignorant folks, that did not know how to be Christians. What I mean is, that there is no place besides Heaven and Hell. These two places will receive all mankind; for Christ says, there are but two sorts, *he that is not with me is against me; and he that gathereth not with me, scattereth abroad.* – The Bible likewise tells us that this world, and all things in it, shall be burnt up – and that "God has appointed a day in which he will judge the world; and that he will bring every secret thing, whether it be good or bad, into judgment – that which is done in secret shall be declared on the house top." I do not know, nor do I think any can tell, but that the day of judgment may last a thousand years. God could tell the state of all his creatures in a moment, but then every thing that every one has done, through his whole life, is to be told before the whole world of angels and men. Oh how solemn is the thought! You and I must stand, and hear every thing we have thought or done, however secret, however wicked and vile, told before all the men and women that ever have been, or ever will be, and before all the angels, good and bad.

Now, my dear friends, seeing the Bible is the word of God, and every thing in it is true, and it reveals such awful and glorious things, what can be more important than that you should learn to read it; and when you have learned to read, that you should study it day and night. There are some things very encouraging in God's word for such ignorant creatures as we are; for God hath not chosen the rich of this world. Not many rich, not many noble are called, but God hath chosen the weak things of this world, and things which are not, to confound the things that are. And when the great and the rich refused coming to the gospel feast, the servant was told to go into the highways and hedges, and compel those poor creatures that he found there, to come in. Now, my brethren, it seems to me that there are no people that ought to attend to the hope of happiness in another world so much as we. Most of us are cut off from comfort and happiness here in this world, and can expect nothing from it. Now seeing this is the case, why should we not take care to be happy after death? Why should we spend our whole lives in sinning against God; and be miserable in this world, and in the world to come? If we do thus, we shall certainly be the greatest fools. We shall be slaves here, and slaves for ever. We cannot plead so great temptations to neglect religion as others. Riches and honours which drown the greatest part of mankind, who have the gospel, in perdition can be little or no temptations to us.

We have so little time in this world that it is no matter how wretched and miserable we are, if it prepares us for Heaven. What is forty, fifty, or sixty years, when compared to eternity? When thousands and millions of years have rolled away, this eternity will be no nigher coming to an end. Oh how glorious is an eternal life of happiness! And how dreadful an eternity of misery! Those of us who have had religious matters, and have been taught to read the Bible, and have been brought by their example and teaching to a sense of divine things, how happy shall we be to meet them in Heaven, where we shall join them in praising God for ever. But if any of us have had such masters, and yet have lived and died wicked, how will it add to our misery to think of our folly. If any of us, who have wicked and profane masters, should become religious, how will our estates be changed in another world. Oh, my friends, let me intreat of you to think on these things, and to live as if you believed them to be true. If you become Christians, you will have reason to bless God for ever, that you have been brought into a land where you have heard the gospel, though you have been slaves. If we should ever get to Heaven, we shall find nobody to reproach us for being black, or for being slaves. Let me beg of you, my dear African brethren, to think very little of your bondage in this life; for your thinking of it will do you no good. If God designs to set us free, he will do it in his own time and way; but think of your bondage to sin and Satan, and do not rest until you are delivered from it.

We cannot be happy, if we are ever so free or ever so rich, while we are servants of sin, and slaves to Satan. We must be miserable here, and to all eternity.

I will conclude what I have to say with a few words to those Negroes who have their liberty. The most of what I have said to those who are slaves, may be of use to you; but you have more advantages, on some accounts, if you will improve your freedom, as you may do, than they. You have more time to read God's holy word, and to take care of the salvation of your souls. Let me beg of you to spend your time in this way, or it will be better for you if you had always been slaves. If you think seriously of the matter, you must conclude that if you do not use your freedom to promote the salvation of your souls, it will not be of any lasting good to you. Besides all this, if you are idle, and take to bad courses, you will hurt those of your brethren who are slaves, and do all in your power to prevent their being free. One great reason that is given by some for not freeing us, I understand, is, that we should not know how to take care of ourselves, and should take to bad courses; that we should be lazy and idle, and get drunk and steal. Now all those of you who follow any bad courses, and who do not take care to get an honest living by your labour and industry, are doing more to prevent our being free than any body else. Let me beg of you then, for the sake of your own good and happiness, in time, and for eternity, and for the sake of your poor brethren, who are still in bondage, *"to lead quiet and peaceable lives in all Godliness and honesty,"* and may God bless you, and bring you to his kingdom, for Christ's sake, Amen.

CHAPTER 18

CELEBRATE BLACK POETRY DAY!

Stanley A. Ransom, Retired Director
Clinton-Essex-Franklin Library System

IN 1965, WHILE Director of the Huntington Public Library, on Long Island's North Shore, I kept finding references to one Jupiter Hamon, an 18th century Black slave poet belonging to Henry Lloyd, who resided on Lloyd's Neck, a community and peninsula just north of Huntington Village. Seeking to learn more about this man, I researched his writings in local libraries, the Long Island Historical Society, the New York Historical Society and the Connecticut Historical Society.. Out of this came a book, "America's First Negro Poet; Jupiter Hammon of Long Island," published in May, 1970, by Kennikat Press of Port Washington, NY.

These were the known complete writings of Jupiter Hammon and also a compilation of earlier writings about him which Kennikat Press had previously published. The term "Negro" was used in the title rather than "Black," after consultation which local Black leaders, who informed me that "Black" was a pejorative term. The book soon sold out, and a second edition was issued in 1983 by Associated Faculty Press, a division of Kraus Reprint, now Barnes and Noble. . My book received a Certificate of Commendation from the American

Association for State and Local History.

The book uncovered the date of Hammon's birth, October 17, 1711 and noted that Hammon's first poem, entitled "An Evening Thought, " was dated December 25, 1760, some ten years prior to poems composed by another Black poet, Phyllis Wheatley. Hammon, in fact, was not only aware of her verse, but he composed a poem addressed to her in 1778. Some of Hammon's poetry, mostly religious, was composed in Hartford, Connecticut, where Hammon's patriot master had fled during the Revolutionary War, when Long Island was occupied by British forces. Later I found that Hammon was manumitted in 1795, moved to Huntington Village, and died about 1805 in Huntington.

Upon the demise of his master, Hammon became the property of John Lloyd, a Loyalist, and returned back to Lloyd Neck in Huntington, then occupied by British troops. Hammon was well read, having been educated with the Lloyd children, and his friends assisted in the publication of his poems. By a remarkable coincidence, my seventh great-grandfather, Reverend Solomon Stoddard of Northampton, Massachusetts, and first Librarian of Harvard College in 1666, was the author of one of the works quoted by Jupiter Hammon in "An Evening's Improvement," a prose sermon published in 1783.

In 1970 I proposed the establishment of Black Poetry Day annually on October 17th with this purpose: "To recognize the contributions of Black poets to American life and culture and to honor Jupiter Hammon, first Black in America to publish his own verse." As Nikki Giovanni has said, "Poetry is part of the strong oral tradition of Black people." Julius Lester also said, "Poetry is the major expression of Black experience."

In Huntington there was a growing concern for the status and well-being of Black members of the community. I helped work to support the Huntington Freedom Center, a source of information, advocacy, voting and assistance to the Black community. As The Connecticut Peddler, my folksinging alter ego, I performed concerts to benefit the Freedom Center.

At the Huntington Public Library a Black Poetry Day Committee was formed, chaired by our Black reference librarian, Arlene Straughn, and including members of the staff. The six public libraries of Huntington Township at Cold Spring Harbor, Huntington, Northport, Commack, Half Hollow Hills and South Huntington got together to promote the first celebration of Black Poetry Week, October 11 to 17th, 1970. Our Huntington Supervisor, Jerome A. Ambro, issued the first Proclamation proclaiming the date of October 17th as "Black Poetry Day" and asking "all citizens to recognize the need for and the unique contribution of the Black poets in our society." The Performing Arts Foundation of Huntington presented "Readings from the Black Poets" on Friday, October 16th at the Huntington Public Library. The observance of Black Poetry Day continued for the next three years, with the Long Island based poet, June Jordan, as the guest speaker on Sunday, October 17th, 1971, and with funding from Poets and Writers, Inc., who are funded by the New York State Council on the Arts. Jerome A. Ambro continued to issue proclamations, at our request, proclaiming October 17th as "Black Poetry Day in Huntington."

I received permission in 1971 to use and publish a poem by Alicia Loy Johnson from the book, "Nine Black Poets," Moore Publishing Company, 1968, called "Black Poetry Day."

"I am waiting for
a day when thousands
will gather before
shops and stores.
I am waiting for
A day when thousands
Of BLACKS will listen
To the words of BLACK POETS.
I am waiting for
A BLACK POETRY DAY."

We made this into many bookmarks and distributed them widely, along with a Bibliography of notable Black Poetry books, many from our library collection. We urged other libraries throughout the State to celebrate Black Poetry Day, and we provided copies of the bookmark and bibliography. Later we heard that in 1985 the State of Oregon had adopted Black Poetry Day as a day of observance in Oregon schools and public places. How wonderful it would be if every state in the Union adopted October 17th as Black Poetry Day! Please ask your state legislature to do it.

In 1974, I became the Director of the Clinton-Essex-Franklin Public Library System, based in Plattsburgh, in upstate New York. With this new job I could not devote the time to promote Black Poetry Day extensively. I did lecture on several occasions in Long Island libraries, in the North Country, and for the New York Library Association's Ethnic Services Round Table (ESRT) on Jupiter Hammon and his poetry and urged the observance of Black Poetry Day. I then formed and chaired another Black Poetry Day Committee, and we applied to the New York State Council on the Arts for annual funding. The committee was enlarged to include community and Black leaders in the Plattsburgh area. My first wife Dorothy, the mother of our three children, died in 1979. In 1980 my new marriage to Christina joined our children and me with a bi-racial family, and our daughter, Shani Aisha Darden, is now a noted esthetician in Hollywood, which gave me an additional reason to promote this special day.

The CEF Library System produced a selected bibliography on "Black American Poetry," a Black Poetry Day bookmark, a sample Proclamation, and a flyer describing Jupiter Hammon and his contribution. Information was sent to "Chase's Calendar of Events; the Day-by-Day Directory to Special Days, Weeks and Months," published annually by Contemporary Books, Chicago, Illinois. This announcement brought requests for information and copies of materials from many libraries and military establishments throughout the country and in military installations in Germany. Our bibliography was adopted by the NAACP in Massachusetts, and in several communities was used by local schools in celebration of Black History Month and in appreciation of Black culture. We sent materials to the San Diego School System and many other schools. Funding was obtained to continue the promotion from the New York State Council on the Arts, From Plattsburgh Air Force Base, and from the Plattsburgh State University College, especially their Multicultural Affairs Committee and from community groups, such as the Dr. Martin Luther King Jr. Commission of Plattsburgh. We also involved the Black and Hispanic college student organizations.

During the 1980's we also commissioned several Black Poetry Day posters, done by Plattsburgh State faculty member Rick Salzman, which were sent to our 29 member libraries and to any interested schools and groups. These outstanding colorful posters were awarded prizes by the Strathmore Paper Company.

I retired in November, 1991 and continue to be on the Black Poetry Day Committee. The Chair of this committee has included Janet Saunders, Marlene Fields, Dr. Michele Carpentier and the current Chair, Dr. Alexis Levitin, who initiated the alliance between the Clinton-Essex-Franklin Library System and the Plattsburgh State University and has been a constant member of the Committee for 33 years.

Dr. Levitin worked to set up our Black Poetry Day as an annual event. He was the one who knew the available Black Poets and he contacted the best poets and raised the funds needed. He also introduces the Black Poetry Day speakers to the Krinovitz Hall audience, which includes students, faculty and members of the Plattsburgh community. Dr. Tracie Church Guzzio from the English Department and I are also on the current Black Poetry Day Committee. Other members of the Black Poetry Day Committee have included Dr. Thomas Braga, artist Steve Booker, Sara Richman, and Robin Caudell, a reporter for the local Plattsburgh Press Republican, who interviewed Black poets chosen for our programs. In 1991 the celebration of Black Poetry Day was proclaimed by New York State Governor Mario Cuomo. We have been supported by the College and by the New York State Council on the Arts, especially Poets & Writers.

We meet for Black Poetry Day programs in the College's Krinovitz Hall. The College obtains a supply of the speaker's books, often at a small discount, to make them available to students and the public.

Our audiences average about 150 persons, many coming from all over the North Country in addition to students and local residents. The accompanying list gives our list of speakers. In 1985 Gwendolyn Brooks from Chicago drew 225 people. She also visited our State Correctional "Facility at Dannemora, NY, where she entranced one hundred inmates, many of them trying to write poetry. In 1992, we had engaged Derek Walcott to speak. The announcement of his Nobel Prize in Literature award came the week before he was to speak, and we held our breath that his entry into clamorous fame would not disturb his schedule. He arrived on time with great local fanfare and read poetry to more than 600 students and community members. It is a great day when Black poetry can attract 600 listeners! Black Poetry Day is a wonderful way to link all parts of the community. Plattsburgh State is making plans to open a Black Poetry Day Center at the college to promote the observance locally and nationally, and will be continuing to invite Black poets to speak at Black Poetry Day. We expect to be able to offer information on Black poets, together with bibliographies, bookmarks, proclamations and posters, and other items for libraries and groups to use in promoting Black Poetry Day.

Black Poetry Day Observance: Librarians, instructors and group leaders usually focus on books and web sites that highlight the works of African-American Poets both past and present, such as Paul Laurence Dunbar, James Weldon Johnson, Gwendolyn Brooks, Langston Hughes, Sonia Sanchez, Nikki Giovanni, Maya Angelou, Camille T. Dungy, Marilyn Nelson, Lucille Clifton, and books such as "Notes on the peanut," by June Jordan, "Tending," and "Still I Rise," and "I Am the Darker Brother." Students should be encouraged to express themselves through poetry and also to read aloud the works by Black poets.

We hope that libraries, schools, colleges and military installations and other venues across the country will decide to celebrate Black Poetry Day as a special day of observance in their communities. As Alicia Loy Johnson has said, "I am waiting for a BLACK POETRY DAY!"

BLACK POETRY DAY SPEAKERS, Plattsburgh, NY

Black Poetry Day is celebrated on or close to October 17th, the birthday of Jupiter Hammon, first Black in America to publish his own verses. "An Evening Thought," published Dec. 25, 1760. Black Poetry Day first celebrated October 16, 1970, at Huntington Public Library, Huntington, NY.

1970: Library Program: Performing Arts Fdn. of Huntington: Selected Readings from Black Poets

1971: June Jordan, Black Poet from Amagansett, Long Island
Hiatus in the celebration, 1972-1977. 1978-83, Celebrated at CEF Lib. Syst., Plattsburgh, NY

1984: June Jordan (First Plattsburgh Observance). PSUC Black Poetry Day Committee formed.

1985: Gwendolyn Brooks; Linda Cousins

1986: Sam Cornish

1987: Nikki Giovanni

1988: Imari Baraka (aka Leroy Jones)

1989: Bernard Finney

1990: Quincy Troupe

1991: Lucille Clifton

1992: Derek Walcott (one week after winning the Nobel Prize for Literature) 600 in attendance

1993: Ntozake Shange

1994: Michael Harper

1995: Jusef Koumanyaka

1996: Jackie Warren-Moore

1997: Allison Joseph

1998: Cornelius Eady

1999: Kevin Young

2000: Tim Seibles

2001: Dennis Brutus

2002: E. Ethelbert Miller

2003: Honoree Fanone Jeffers

2004: A. van Jordan
2005: Tony Medina
2006: Marilyn Nelson (Poet Laureate of Connecticut)
2007: Aracelis Girmay
2008: Major Jackson
2009: LaTasha Nevada Diggs
2010: Thomas Sayers Ellis
2011: Dr. Gretna Wilkinson
2012: Dr. Charles Fort
2013: Amber Flora Thomas
2014: Jericho Brown
2015: Gregory Pardlo (2015 Pulitzer Prize for Poetry) 130 in audience
2016: Camille T. Dungy
2017: Rickey Levantiis
2018: Ladan Osnan
2019: Dr. Kwame Dawes

Stanley A. Ransom first published in 1970 and 1983 his book: "America's First Negro Poet; Jupiter Hammon of Long Island," containing all the works found up to that time.

CHAPTER 19

MUSIC ON LONG ISLAND

MUSIC WAS VERY much evident on Long Island in the 17th and 18th centuries. Cities and towns had local bands, often military bands which played music for the citizens. Taverns had musicians who played for customers or for dances. Private homes often had violins, fiddles, spinets and melodions, flutes, drums and guitars and other stringed instruments, and many families enjoyed singing. Churches offered sacred music. What then of the Lloyd Family and the families at Queen's Village at Lloyd Neck?

Of course the Lloyd family, being Anglican, went to church on Sunday. They even sailed across Long Island Sound in their boat, "Wentworth" to worship at the Anglican High Church at Stamford, Connecticut. Probably the Lloyds and servants would sing the hymns and sing the responses. Henry Lloyd was a strong supporter of the church. One of the things I have liked about the Episcopal service was the singing of responses. When I was attending Columbia University, my wife and I would walk across 110th Street on Sunday to St. John's Episcopal Cathedral, which offered a boys' choir and a chance to sing the hymns and responses.

But of the Lloyd Family on Long Island, there seems to be no record or mention of any music or even any musical instruments. The papers of the Lloyd family contain much about business and family but no mention was made of music playing or singing. According to SPLIA archeologist Jenna Coplin, PhD, there was no mention of music instruments in any of the wills or inventories. A curious lack.

Russel B. Nye, writing about Jupiter's poetry in the Long Island Forum for June, 1940, notes, "Hammon probably followed the example and tradition of Isaac Watts, the Methodist Hymn writer, who died in 1748." Other writers have noticed the similarity of Jupiter's verses to hymns.

Vernon Loggins states" Like the spirituals, the poems of Jupiter Hammon were composed to be heard." "He uses a verse form which is found in the early Methodist hymns." "There are many examples of syncopation, so characteristic of Negro dance rhythms."

Poetry has deep roots in music. Both have rhythms and tempo, and poems are a blend of sound and music. Included here are two music pieces I composed for Jupiter Hammon: "Jupiter Hammon's Jig," and music for "An Address to Miss Phillis Wheatley," in a chorus or Gospel style that would be acceptable to accompany Hammon's poetry.

I appreciate the good work of Shirley Baird, a musician and retired college professor from Kingston, Ontario, who has arranged the "Address" for use by choruses and has arranged "Jupiter's Jig" as a separate piece of music to perform.

"Jupiter Hammon's Jig" will be useful for college and community string bands, single performers, or folk groups to perform. It can be heard on YouTube under the title.

The "Address to Miss Phillis Wheatley" can be used by college or community choruses and especially by Gospel Choirs to offer Jupiter's religious poetry in a new way. The twenty-one verses of this work have been shortened to six, but more of his verses are available in this work if needed.

Note that both compositions have been copyrighted. They can be performed without charge if credit is given to composer and arranger:

"Address to Miss Phillis Wheatley, Composed by Stanley A Ransom Jr. and arranged by Shirley Baird. Copyright 2005."

"Jupiter Hammon's Jig, Composed by Stanley A. Ransom Jr. and arranged by Shirley Baird. Copyright 2018."

In many people's lives, music is an essential element. As a part-time professional musician, singer songwriter and storyteller, I can attest to this fact. Music thrives on college campuses and communities across America and goes hand in hand with poetry and poetic expression. These compositions may help bring attention to Jupiter Hammon and his life and poetry.

Stanley Austin Ransom Jr.

CHAPTER 20

MUSIC TO PERFORM:
HAMMON AND WHEATLEY

Score

Jupiter Hammon's Jig

Jupiter Hammon, 1711-1805

Stanley Austin Ransom
Arranger: Shirley Baird

(Complete Phillis Wheatley poem to sing for Choirs, 21 verses)
(Six verse poem to sing for Choirs)
AN ADDRESS TO
MISS PHILLIS WHEATLEY

I

O come you pious youth! Adore
The wisdom of thy God,
In bringing thee from distant shore
To learn His holy word.

Eccles. xii.

II

Thou mightst been left behind
Amidst a dark abode;
God's tender mercy still combin'd,
Thou hast the holy word.

Psal. cxxxv. 2, 3.

IV

God's tender mercy brought thee here;
Tost o'er the raging main;
In Christian faith thou hast a share,
Worth all the gold of Spain.

Psal. ciii, 1, 3, 4.

V

While thousands tossed by the sea,
And others settled down,
God's tender mercy set thee free,
From dangers that come down.

Death.

VI

That thou a pattern still might be,
To youth of Boston town,
The blessed Jesus set thee free,
From every sinful wound.

2 Cor. v. 10.

XXI

Now glory be to the Most High,
United praises given,
By all on earth, incessantly,
And all the host of heav'n.

Psal. cl. 6.

Address To Miss Phillis Wheatley

Composer Stanley A Ransom Jr © 2005
Arranged by Shirley Baird

Lyrics by Jupiter Hammon (1711-1805)

O come you pi - youth! a - dore The wis - dom of thy God

In bring - ing thee from dis - tant shore To learn His hol - word

Thou misght - st have been left be - hind a - midst a dark a - bode

God's ten - der mer - cy still com - bin'd thou hast the ho - ly word

Stanley A Ransom Jr 2005

CHAPTER 21

BIBLIOGRAPHY OF THE WORKS OF JUPITER HAMMON, BY OSCAR WEGELIN

WITH TWO NEW Poems Added by S. Ransom

An / Evening Thought. / Salvation by Christ, / with / Penetential Cries: / Composed by Jupiter Hammon, a Negro belonging to Mr. Lloyd, of Queen's- / Village, on Long-Island, the 25th of December, 1760. / Broadside of 88 lines, printed in double column, and the word "Finis" at bottom. Size 10-1/4 x 7-7/8 inches.

> This broadside proves conclusively that Jupiter Hammon was writing poetry in America at least nine years before Phillis Wheatley published her first work, The elegy on the death of Whitefield. It also proves that Hammon was without doubt the first writer of color whose work appeared in print in what is now the United States. The only copy known is in The New York Historical Society. It was probably printed at New York.

"Sickness, Death and Funeral" / Poem composed by Jupiter Hammon / A Negro belonging to Mr. Joseph Lloyd / of Queen's Village on Long Island / August the 10th 1770 / Phebe Townsend.

> Addressed to: "Come all ye youth of Boston Town," the 72 line poem by Jupiter Hammon, transcribed by Phebe Townsend (1763-1841) of Raynham Hall, Oysterbay, NY. Handwritten in three sections. Found in Townsend Family Papers, Patricia D. Klingenstein Library, New-York Historical Society by independent Scholar Claire Bellerjeau in 2015. (S. Ransom)

Address to Miss Phillis Wheatly (*sic*):
Hartford, August 4, 1778. / An Address to Miss Phillis Wheatly, *(sic)* Ethiopian Po- / etess, in Boston, who came from Africa at eight years of age, and / soon became acquainted with the Gospel of Jesus Christ. / (one line, followed by 21 verses of 4 lines each, printed in double column) / Composed by Jupiter Hammon, a Negro Man belonging to Mr. Joseph Lloyd, of Queen's Village, / on Long-Island, now in Hartford. /

> The above lines are published by the Author, and a number of his friends, who desire to join with him in their best / regards to Miss Wheatly *(sic)* / Broadside, without doubt printed at Hartford. Size 8-3/4 x 6 inches. The only known copy is in the Connecticut Historical Society.

An Essay on the ten Virgins. Composed by Jupiter Hammon, a Negro Man belonging To Mr. Joseph Lloyd of Queen's Village on Long Island, now in Hartford. Hartford: Printed by Hudson and Goodwin, 1779.

> I have been unable to locate a copy of the above. It is mentioned in the Conn. Courant, Dec. 14, 1779. "To be sold at the Printing-Office in Hartford." Although mentioned by several bibliographers, none give a collation and All seem to take their information from the above source, or from Trumbull's list of Conn. Imprints. Mr. Trumbull also obtained his information from the advertisement in the *Courant*.

An / Evening's Improvement. / Shewing, / the Necessity of beholding / the Lamb of God. / *to which is added.* / A Dialogue, / Entitled, / The Kind Master and / Dutiful Servant. / Written by Jupiter Hammon, a Negro / Man belonging to Mr. John Lloyd, of Queen's / Village, on Long-Island, now in Hartford. / Hartford: / *Printed for the Author, by the Assistance of his Friends.* / 8vo. pp. (2),-3-28. [1779].

> Printed during the Revolution, probably by Hudson & Goodwin. The New York Historical Society has the copy formerly owned by Daniel Parish, Jr.
>
> This is the only copy I can trace.

A / Winter Piece: / being a / Serious Exhortation, with a call to the / Unconverted: / and a short / Contemplation / on the / Death of Jesus Christ. / Written by Jupiter Hammon, / A Negro Man belonging to Mr. John Lloyd, of / Queen's Village, on Long Island, now in Hartford. / Published by the Author with the Assistance / of his Friends. / Hartford: / Printed for the Author. / M. DCC. LXXXII: (1782) / 8vo. pp. (2),-22-(1),-24.

> Probably printed by Hudson & Goodwin. "A Poem for children with Thoughts on Death." Occupies pp. (23)-24. Copies are in The Connecticut Historical Society and in The Massachusetts Historical Society Collections. Another is in the Providence Public Library. 1782.

An Essay on Slavery, with Submission to Divine Providence, knowing that God Rules over all things. Written by Jupiter Hammon and in his hand. Composed of 25 four line verses. Dated November 10, 1786. This is a year before he published his "Address to the Negroes of the State of New-York." "Composed by Jupiter Hammon A Negro Man belonging to Mr. John Lloyd Queen's Village on Long Island. November 10, 1786."

> This important poem was discovered in 2011 by Julie McCown, graduate student of Dr. Cedric May, among the Hillhouse Family Papers in Sterling Memorial Library at Yale

University. The poem discusses slavery and freedom:

Verse 17:
> "Come let us join with humble voice
> Now on the Christian shore.
> If we will have our only choice
> 'Tis slavery no more."   (S. Ransom)

An / Address / to the / Negroes / In the State of New-York, / By Jupiter Hammon, / Servant of John Lloyd, jn, Esq; of the Manor of Queen's Village, Long-Island. / (4 lines from Acts. X. 34, 35) / New-York: / Printed by Carroll and Patterson / No. 32, Maiden-Lane, / M, DCC, LXXXVII. / 8vo pp. (2), -III, -IV, -(1), -6-20.

A copy is in the collection of Henry C. Sturges, of New York. Others are in The New York Historical Society and in The John Carter Brown Library.

The Printers of this, the first edition, make the following statement, the wording differing slightly from that in the Philadelphia re-issue:

"As this Address is wrote in a better stile than could be expected from a slave, some may doubt of the genuineness of the Production. The author, as he informs in the title page, is a servant of Mr. Lloyd, and has been remarkable for his fidelity and abstinence from those vices, which he warns his brethren against. The manuscript wrote in his own hand, is in our possession. We have made no material alterations in it, except in the spelling, which we found needed considerable correction.

The Printers,
New-York 20th. Feb. 1787.

An / Address / to the Negroes, / In The / State of New-York. / by Jupiter Hammon, Servant of John Lloyd, / jun. Esq. of the Manor of Queen's Village, Long-Island. / (3 lines from *Acts*. X. 34, 35. /

New-York Printed: / Philadelphia Reprinted By Daniel Humphreys, / in Spruce-Street, near the Drawbridge. / M. DCC. LXXXVII. / 8vo. pp. (3),-4-15,-(1).

Dedicated "To the Members of the African Society of New York." Dated "Queen's Village, 24th. Sept. 1786." On the last page is the following interesting statement: "As this address is wrote in a better stile than could be expected from a slave, some may be ready to doubt of the genuineness of the production. – The Author, as he informs in the title-page, is a servant of Mr. Lloyd, and has been remarkable for his fidelity and abstinence from those vices, which he warns his brethren against. The manuscript wrote in his own hand, is in the possession of Messrs. Carroll and Patterson, printers, in New-York. – They have made no material alterations in it, except in the spelling, which they found needed considerable correction. The Printer."

Copies of this edition are in the New York Public Library and in the Harvard College Library. A copy in the New York Historical Society has a leaf preceding the title which contains the following statement. This copy is the only one I have been able to trace which has this leaf.

"At a Meeting of the Acting Committee of the Pennsylvania Society for Promoting the Abolition of Slavery, &c. June 30, 1787 – A Pamphlet wrote by Jupiter Hammon, servant to John Lloyd, jun. Esq. Queen's Village, Long-Island, and addressed to the African descendants in General, was laid before them.

Impressed with a lively sense of the good effects that may result from a re-publication therof, to those persons to whom it is particularly addressed, Ordered, that Daniel Humphreys be directed to print five hundred copies, for the purposes above mentioned.

Extract from the Minutes.
Thomas Harrison, Clerk to
Acting Committee."

An Address to the Negroes in the State of New York. By Jupiter Hammon. New York: 1806. 12 mo. Pp.22.

> The compiler of this list had a copy of this edition several years ago. It was printed after Hammon's death and contains an attestation by three residents of Oyster Bay as to the author's good character. Although the latest of the three known editions, it seems to be the most difficult to locate. A copy was in the New York State Library but was destroyed by the fire of 1911.

CHAPTER 22

JUPITER HAMMON BIBLIOGRAPHY

Stanley A. Ransom, Jr.

African American Historic Designation Council. Tribute to Jupiter Hammon. Booklet 4, Town of Huntington, February, 2011.

Bailey, Rosalie Fellows. The Account Books of Henry Lloyd. In: The Journal of Long Island History, Vol. 2, No. 1, p. 26-49, Spring, 1962.

Barck, Dorothy C., Editor. Papers of the Lloyd Family. 2 vols. 1927, the New York Historical Society, c1927.

Bolton, Charla E. and Reginald H. Metcalf. The Migration of Jupiter Hammon and His Family: From Slavery to Freedom and its Consequences. In: Long Island History, Vol. 23, Issue 2, 2013. 16 p. Their amazing research resulted in the best description of Jupiter and his family.

Bowen, George Loveridge, M.D., A Condensed History of the Lloyd Family of Lloyd Neck, presented at the Huntington Historical Society in the Spring of 1982. In Huntington Historical Society Quarterly, volume 21, Number 3, Spring, 1982. Pp. 9-28.

Bowen, George Loveridge. James Lloyd II, M.D. And His Family on Lloyd Neck. c1988 by George Loveridge Bowen. Privately Printed. 222 p.

Brucia, Margaret A. The African-American Poet, Jupiter Hammon: A Home-born Slave and his Classical Name, In: International Journal of the Classical Tradition, Vol. 7, No. 4, Spring 2001, pp 515-522.

Buell, Rev. Samuel. A Faithful Narrative of the Remarkable Revival of Religion in the Congregation of EastHampton, on Long-Island, in the year of our Lord, 1764... And also an Account of the Revival of Religion in Bridgehampton & Easthampton in the year 1800. Printed by Alden Spooner, Sag-Harbor [NY] 1803. 144p.

Clark, Margaret Goff. Jupiter Hammon; America's First Black Poet in Print. p. 11-37. In: Clark, M. G., Their Eyes on the Stars; Four Black Writers. Toward Freedom Series, Juvenile literature. c1973 Margaret Goff Clark. Garrard Publishing Company, Champlain, IL.

Coplin, Jenna Wallace, Ed. Mapping African American History Across Long Island. In: Long Island History Journal, 2013, Volume 23, Issue 2. 18p.

Day, Lynda R. Making a Way to Freedom; A History of African Americans on Long Island. c1997, Long Island Studies Institute, Hofstra University. Empire State Books, Interlaken, New York. 160p.

Flint, Martha Bockee. Early Long Island; A Colonial Study. G.P. Putman's Sons, c1896. History of Lloyd's Neck and Long Island during the American Revolution.

Griswold, Mac. The Manor; Three Centuries at a Slave Plantation on Long Island. c2013 Mac Griswold. Picador; Farrar, Straus and Giroux, New York. 461 p.

Hall, Courtney R. Some Impressions of Flushing. In: the Journal of Long Island History, Vol. 1, No. 1, p. 21-32, Spring, 1961.

Hayes, Katherine Howlett. Slavery Before Race; Europeans, Africans, and Indians at Long Island's Sylvester Manor Plantation, 1651-1884. c2013, New York University Press, New York and London. 220p.

Heartman, Charles Frederick. Phillis Wheatley (Phillis Peters). A Critical Attempt and a Bibliography of Her Writings. Facsimile Publisher, NY, 1915. 65 p. Contains on page 64 a note about Jupiter Hammon's 21 verse poem to her, along with best wishes to her.

Kaplan, Sidney and Emma Nogrady Kaplan. Jupiter Hammon, In: The Black Presence in the Era of the American Revolution, Revised Edition, c1989, The University of Massachusetts Press, Amherst, MA. p. 191-200.

Knight, Helen C. Lady Huntington and Her Friends, or the Revival of the Work of God in the Days of Wesley, Whitefield, Romaine, Venn and others in the Last Century. 1853, American Tract Society, NY, NY. Rev. Whitefield and the religious revival on Long Island. 292 p.

Kobrin, David. The Black Minority in Early New York. The NY State Education Department. Office of State History, Albany, 1971. 45 p.

Lloyd, Henry. An Old Long Island Map, Henry Lloyd's Scrapbook, 1835-1850. Compiled by Theodore Lyman Frost, Huntington Public Library, Huntington, NY.

Lloyd, Mrs. Mary. Meditations on Divine Subjects; to Which is Prefixed, an Account of Her Life and Character, by E. Pemberton. J. Parker, New York, 1750. 57 p.

May, Cedrick, and Julie McCown. An Essay on Slavery: An Unpublished Poem by Jupiter Hammon, In: Early American Literature, Vol. 48, No. 2, 2013, p. 457-471.

May, Cedrick, Jupiter Hammon. Early Minority Literature, 1/10/2018, 19p.

May, Cedrick. The Collected Works of Jupiter Hammon; Poems and Essays. University of Tennessee Press, 2017. 93 p.

Maybee, Carlton. Black Education in New York State: From Colonial to Modern Times, 1979

McGee, Dorothy Horton. Raynham Hall, 1738-1960. c1960 by Dorothy Horton McGee. 1961, Town of Oyster Bay, NY. 28 p. Reprinted from the Nassau County Historical Journal, Vol. 21, Nos. 3 and 4, c1960, Myron H. Luke, PhD, Editor.

Moss, Richard Shannon. Slavery on Long Island; A Study in Local Institutional and Early African-American Communal Life. Garland Publishing, Inc. New York and London, c1993. 249 p.

Napper, Emily Foster. The First Negro Poet of America. In: The Literary Collector; An Illustrated Monthly Magazine of Book-Lore and Bibliography, V. 8, No. 3, July, 1904, p. 73-76.

Naylor, Natalie A., Editor. Exploring African-American History; Long Island and Beyond. Long Island Studies Institute, Hofstra University, Hempstead, NY. page 8. c1991.

Nydam, Arlen. Numerological Tradition in the Works of Jupiter Hammon. In: African American Review, Vol. 40, No. 2, p. 207-220, Summer, 2006. "Hammon's use of number symbolism and multiple layers of meaning."

Nye, Russel B. America's First Negro Poet. Long Island Forum, June, 1940, P. 129-30.

O'Neale, Sondra A. Jupiter Hammon of Long Island: America's First Black Writer. p. 119-128. In: Krieg, Joann P., Editor, Evoking a Sense of Place (Long Island Studies), Heart of the Lakes Publishing, Interlaken, NY, 1988. C1988, Long Island Studies Institute, Hofstra University, Hempstead, NY.

O'Neale, Sondra A. Jupiter Hammon and The Biblical Beginnings of African-American Literature. ATLA Monograph Series, No. 28. c1993 by Sondra A. O'Neale. The American Theological Library Association and the Scarecrow Press, Inc., 1993. 291 p.

Osann, Jean B. Henry Lloyd's Salt Box Manor House. c1978; Revised Edition, c1982, Jean B. Osann. The Printer, Huntington, NY.

Overton, Jacqueline. Long Island's Story, with a Sequel, the Rest of the Story, 1929-1961, by Bernice Marshall. Garden City, Doubleday, Doran & Co., 1929 and Ira J. Friedman, Inc., Port Washington, NY, c1961. 348p. & 44p.

Perkins, Nathan. A Sermon Occasioned by the Unhappy Death of Mr. Lloyd: a Refugee from Long Island. 1780, Hartford, Hudson & Goodwin.

Prime, Nathaniel S. A History of Long Island, from its first settlement by Europeans to the year 1845, with Special Reference to its Ecclesiastical Concerns. Robert Carter, NY, 1845. 420 p.

Ransom, Stanley Austin. America's First Negro Poet; The Complete Works of Jupiter Hammon of Long Island. Kennikat Press. 1970. 2nd edition, Associated Faculty Press, 1983.

Records of the First Church of Huntington, LI, NY. CD by Long Island Genealogy, c2003.

Redding, J. Saunders, To Make a Poet Black, Chapel Hill, University of North Carolina Press, c1939. 142 p.

Reese, Carolyn. From Jupiter Hammon to LeRoi Jones. In: Changing Education, Fall, 1966. p. 30-34.

Richards, Phillip M. Nationalist Themes in the Preaching of Jupiter Hammon. In: Early American Literature, Vol. 25, No. 2, 1990. pp. 123-138.

Sammis, Romanah, Editor. Huntington-Babylon Town History. Published by Huntington Historical Society, c1937 Huntington Historical Society. 296 p.

Schmidt, Charlotte Lloyd. Memoranda Concerning Lloyd's Neck, Long Island, NY and the Lloyd Family. Privately Printed, 1884.

Schuessleraug, Jennifer. Confronting Slavery at Long Island's Oldest Estates. New York Times, August 12-15, 2015. Descriptions of slave rooms at Joseph Lloyd Manor by Joseph McGill. 12 p.

Scott, Kenneth, and Susan E. Klaffky. A History of the Joseph Lloyd Manor House. c1976. Society for the Preservation of Long Island Antiquities, Setauket, Long Island, NY. 64 p.

Sinha, Manisha. The Slave's Cause; A History of Abolition. c2016, Yale University Press. 784 p. A history of Abolition from Jupiter Hammon's and other slave's point of view. A new look.

Stoddard, Rev. Solomon. The Safety of Appearing at the Day of Judgment in the Righteousness of Christ. 3rd ed. D. Henchman, Boston, 1742. 296 p. Hammon read his books.

Thompson, Benjamin F. History of Long Island; containing An Account of the Discovery and Settlement... E. French, NY, 1839. Lloyd Neck, p. 326-328. 536 p.

Townshend, Charles Hervey. The British Invasion of New Haven, Connecticut, Together with Some Account of their Landing and Burning the Towns of Fairfield and Norwalk, July, 1779. Tuttle, Morehouse & Taylor, 1879.

Valentine, Harriet G. and Andrus T. An Island's People: One Foot in the Sea, One on Shore. Huntington, NY, Peterson Press, c1976.

Vertancs, Charles A. Jupiter Hammon; Early Negro Poet of L.I. In: The Nassau County Historical Journal, Vol. 18, No. 1, Winter, 1957. p1-17.

Wegelin, Oscar. Jupiter Hammon; American Negro Poet, Selections from his Writings and a Bibliography. c1915 by Oscar Wegelin. 51p. No. 48 of 91 copies, Heartman's Historical Series No. 13.

Woolsey, Rev. Melancthon Lloyd. The Lloyd Manor of Queens Village; Address Delivered at the Eleventh Annual Meeting of the New York Branch of the Order of Colonial Lords of Manors in America, Held in the city of New York April 27th, 1923. 28 unnumbered pages. Baltimore, 1925. Reprinted 1951 by the Society for the Preservation of Long Island Antiquities. Map, photos, illustrations.

Henry Lloyd I Salt Box Manor House, 1711.
Courtesy of the Lloyd Harbor Historical Society

Joseph Lloyd 1766 House. Public Domain

Escape Hatch in Joseph Lloyd House, second floor. At end of
Revolutionary War, twelve British soldiers reputed to have escaped to
the shore using this hatch, avoiding the wrath of waiting Patriots.
Photo by Stanley Ransom.

INDEX

Photos and illustrations are indicated by italic page numbers.